MW00442180

LIVING
ABOVE THE
CHAOS

**A Practical Guide to Peak Performance
and Self Mastery in a Crazy World**

Ol Ashton
you are perfect

OWEN THOMAS ASHTON, MD

... Continuing to whack the beehive

Living Above the Chaos
A Practical Guide to Peak Performance and Self Mastery in a Crazy World
By Owen Thomas Ashton, MD

Copyright 2019 Owen Thomas Ashton, MD
Seaworthy Publishing

No part of this publication may be reproduced, stored in a retrieval system, or transmitted in any form or by any means without the prior written permission of the author and publisher except in accordance with the provisions of the Copyright, Designs and Patents Act 1988.

This book is not intended to provide personalized medical, legal, financial or investment advice. The author and the publisher specifically disclaim any liability, loss or risk, personal or otherwise, that is incurred as a consequence, directly or indirectly, of the use and application of any of the contents of this book.

Book Interior and E-book Design by Amit Dey | amitdey2528@gmail.com

ISBN: 978-1692398965

This book is based on the personal observations and experiences of Dr. Owen Thomas Ashton. The author's intent is to offer information of a general nature to help you in your quest for physical, emotional, and spiritual well-being. Any application of the material set forth in the following pages is at the reader's discretion and is his or her sole responsibility. The author and the publisher assume no responsibility for your actions. The stories in this book are all true, but the names have been changed in some circumstances to protect privacy.

To Infinity:
Thanks for Perfection

There is no doubt that mankind is evolving into an era of critical importance. The laws of nature dictate a way. Each person must return to this way for his own benefit and for the benefit of all humanity.

— Owen Thomas Ashton, MD

CONTENTS

Preface

Avoid judgment. You don't have all the facts.

—Owen Thomas Ashton, MD

Are you ready?

"Ready" means receptive. It is a state of mind established by our intent to embrace change and allows us to suspend negativity and surrender our egomania to Infinite Wisdom. This occurs when we turn away from our worn-out belief systems and open the conscious mind to new possibilities.

Surrender your conscious mind to Infinite Wisdom, which dwells within your subconscious mind. Open your mind to outrageous concepts that have thus far escaped your perception. Get ready for a radical departure from "normal." Get ready to enter the realm of Infinite Wisdom and experience unconditional love. The project is you; take charge of your project and be ready to become whole, strong, perfect, powerful, loving, harmonious, and happy.

"Ready" means receptive.

INTRODUCTION

Many interesting and frightful events have entered our awareness recently that have challenged our ability to perceive security and happiness. The world scene is dominated by chaos, local and regional conflicts, economic downturn, unemployment, family disintegration, drug addiction, crime, domestic terror, and the list goes on and on. These words could have been written two years ago, ten years ago, or even three thousand years ago. The point is, life on this planet is chaotic and unpredictable. The "chaos" will always be with us. We must learn to live above the chaos, which is, as the Buddha said, "like the lotus flower, which grows out of muddy water but remains untouched by the mud."

We have witnessed disastrous weather events that have caused massive destruction and injury as the controversy rages as to the causes of global climate change. We have watched wars and conflicts unfold before our eyes. We have experienced ill health and emotional pain in our own lives.

Sometimes we may even doubt our collective abilities to cope. We doubt our abilities to resolve conflict. We doubt that we can end suffering and find true happiness. This indicates that we have not yet accepted into our belief systems a natural law that states, "Everything is perfect." In that regard, we have much to learn. Belief in perfection means that all judgments represent human folly. Belief in perfection means we enter a state of mind that allows the banishment of doubt.

But how can we really accept that perfection is possible in this chaotic collection of events we call life? In the writings that follow, I ask you to be skeptical but receptive. Question these concepts, yes, but open your mind to new avenues of thought that will require you to use your powers of intuition and imagination. These powers represent the core abilities that define our species. These powers define our position in creation as creators of our own destinies.

By whatever means we deem effective for our evolution into enhanced awareness, let us set an intention to become more balanced by paying more attention to our intuition and less time judging events as anything other than the consequences of natural law. Let us refrain from seeking validation from external circumstances and events. This means we must accept responsibility for our own lives. This means we can evaluate our position and know that through our own efforts or lack thereof, we have created life as we presently perceive it to be. We can become aware of how our ego-based perspectives (egomania) have divided humanity into separate and distinct cultural and political camps. Thus, we experience constant conflict, war, and fear.

Natural Law

Up until now, your life has been a joke. Are you offended? Don't be. I mean no disrespect, but your life has been based on a lie. Your life story is a lie, and you made it all up as you went along your merry (and sometimes not-so-merry) way. You made it all up in your domesticated consciousness. You came to false conclusions based on false teachings. You were never told about your innate divinity or your perfection. This divinity in reality defines your true nature, and it is your destiny to discover your true nature.

We live in an illusionary world that seems so real as to make us want to live our lives surrounded by the insanity we call "normal." In this way, we suffer, and in this way, we justify that suffering by accepting what we have always been told to be true. In justifying our suffering, we waste our lives. "Our human lives can indeed be needlessly wasted in a repetition compulsion. Repetition compulsions can be endless unless they are given up by an act of will. Do not make this pathetic human error" (A Course In Miracles, Helen Schucman).

Only through awareness (an act of will) of natural law may we stop wasting our lives. The most significant awareness of natural law that we can achieve is to love ourselves unconditionally. This may seem an impossible task, but in reality, it is not a task at all; it is merely remembering our pristine state of perfection.

So why are we here? What is our purpose on this planet? What can we hope to achieve if we attempt to forge a better understanding of natural law? And how will our lives change if we do so?

In answer to the first question, we are here of our own volition, out of infinity, simply because we must. We must because in infinity everything must. "Infinity" means that every conceivable and inconceivable entity exists without end. And in this particular corner of the universe, we are blessed with this one experience out of innumerable possibilities on planet Earth to create time, motion, matter, change, impermanence, strife, lack, fear, scarcity, hatred, jealousy, greed, etc. (all through our egomania) and then to evolve into acceptance, surrender, forgiveness, compassion, empathy, love, and, finally, unconditional love (a triumph of spirit). This is our purpose on this planet. This is what we can hope to achieve if we forge a better understanding of natural law. And if we can learn to evolve to a life of unconditional love, our lives will change for the better.

From this point forward, our aim will be to exercise our free will to evolve into an enlightened state, an aware state—to become the channel for the universe to express here and now, the latest version of the Infinite Wisdom's greatest vision. We will become more skilled and peaceful as we seek this enlightenment.

But this task seems so large! Enlightenment seems so unattainable! This "seeming" is true; what I ask you to start doing today—to take steps to evolve as a human being—is no easy task on its surface. But you have to remember that enlightenment, peace, and perfection is our natural state. We're not evolving toward some unattainable goal; we're evolving into what we were designed to be! And like any great journey, that evolution must begin with a single thought.

These statements may seem to represent a distant cloud of wishful thinking. They may even make little sense to us at this time. Our understanding of these concepts depends on our level of awareness. In part II of this book, our aim will be to increase our level of awareness, but first, we must gain a fuller understanding of this new perspective in part I. I'm very excited for this journey we're about to take together. It is a journey toward awareness. And in this awareness, we can begin to live above the chaos, like children, like the perfect beings we used to be. The chaos will always be with us, but when we reach a certain level of awareness, we will begin to appreciate even that.

I believe that at the moment of birth into this physical world, every last one of us arrived in a state of spiritual perfection. This might come as a surprise, the idea of human perfection. It might even be a difficult concept for you to accept at first—after all, it's highly likely that you don't remember ever feeling that way. But it's true. On the day of your birth, you were a perfect, new human, suddenly and violently placed into a new world.

Compared to the realm of infinity from which we came, we found this new world to be immediately uncomfortable. For the first time, we experienced the terrifying loneliness of being a separate entity. Until then, we were used to feeling complete, at peace, and as one with Infinite Wisdom. I will get into the nature and meaning of the Infinite Wisdom shortly. For now, what we must consider is that, for all of us, conception was merely an act of Infinite Wisdom, giving us the opportunity to experience this corner of the universe in a physical form.

This rather trite explanation of life might seem a little too simplistic, but the more I ponder this concept, the better I feel. The notion that we are all literally connected to a higher power (and always have been) makes me feel the kind of peace that most people spend lifetimes trying to achieve. For many, obtaining this level of consciousness requires an evolution of our acquired mental state. Most never approach or even seek this awareness. For those who do seek it, most never find it until the moment of physical death. With this writing, I intend to explore profound concepts into this awareness, ultimately arriving at a deeper understanding of the nature of truth. Hopefully, I will help you discover and define it for yourself.

As a brief introduction to the true nature of things, let us review what we know. Although life began on planet earth five hundred million years ago, our true nature was actually established some 14.5 billion years earlier, when our known universe was manifested by an event scientists call the big bang. Later, we will discuss this creation event in more detail, but for now, I assume you have heard about this scientific explanation that is widely accepted as fact.

Geologists have described the many fantastic forms planet Earth took before its present state. All the many horrific events eventually resulted in a planet that was perfectly suited for the establishment of life forms. Life began here five hundred million years ago as forces (yet to be understood), assembled elements from the far reaches of the cosmos.

You are the latest and greatest version of this five hundred millionyear evolutionary process. You are descended from early combinations of elements that began as primitive combinations of carbon and amino acids. Your present physical form (and therefore you) required five hundred million years to evolve. You are indeed fortunate to be here.

If you can wrap your head around these creation concepts, you can become aware of how unique and special you really are. You are the latest version of God's greatest vision. You are unique in so many ways because no other person has had, or ever will have, your exact genetic code and no other person has had, or ever will have, your specific life experience.

Through the lessons that follow, I am confident that you will discover for yourself what is true for you. I am confident that you will increase your level of awareness and perceive your true nature. You will conclude that you are the latest version of God's greatest vision.

You will discover that you are therefore perfect and need not suffer and are capable of giving and receiving unconditional love.

A word of caution: If you think you will uncover the absolute truth here, you are wrong. Absolute truth is one of those unknowable concepts that we innately seek. And although truth is unchanging and immortal, the truth that I perceive may not be meaningful for another. That is the only true statement one can make about the truth. Maybe these lessons will allow you to feel more at home in your own life. Indeed, the reason I started writing was because it made me feel better. Then I discovered that feeling better was my purpose because then I could help others feel better. So I kept writing. After many months of research and discovery, I have come to some key conclusions on the things that appear to be true for me. With the hope that they will help you find your own truth, I offer them to you in this volume.

As you will see in the pages to come, The book is based on scientific and metaphysical principles that uncover the secrets behind our wounding and negative self-talk, ultimately redirecting our perceptions of right/wrong, good/bad, revenge, greed, avarice, scarcity, disunity, self-esteem, forgiveness, and unconditional love. The project (your project) will reveal new findings in the fields of health, fitness, and wellbeing to help you arrive at a new sense of contentment and peace. The truths I intend to share with you in this volume will open your eyes to possibilities you could never have imagined before, and you will be able to shift your orientation from a destructive egomania to one of genuine self-love and mutual compassion. However, you must hold strongly in your awareness that you are the project.

The project is about you. Not your spouse or your kids, your friends or your boss. You. You cannot love anyone or anything until you love yourself unconditionally.

PART I

THE REAL YOU

CHAPTER 1

PERFECT IMPERFECTIONS

L et's start with the day of your birth. As a first attempt to gather what that day must have been like, let's think about your life in the womb. In short, it was nine months of pure bliss and continued comfort. In this phase of your creation, you were still very much connected to the perfection that we all share. There was no reason for you to feel or know anything else.

But then on the day of your birth, all of that changed. Your ideal environment gave way to bright lights, noise, cold, pain, and hunger. This was certainly a jarring experience, but all of these terrifying and troubling new sensations were nothing compared to the notion that overshadowed them all: at the moment of your birth, you began to experience separation from Infinite Wisdom for the first time. No wonder you cried so much. This new human experience was entirely unpleasant.

So on that day of your birth, you began to experience separation. That very unpleasant feeling established the basis of your present state of being. If you were physically nurtured and sustained by caring parents, you survived and thrived in amazing ways. If you were abused or neglected, your separation anxiety multiplied as your perception of reality was ingrained into your subconscious mind.

Unfortunately, the picture did not get any better for as you grew up. After just a few years of interaction with your new environment, you learned another perspective: believing that you are not perfect. You also learned that, no matter what you did, you could never get enough of anything. You learned the opposite of perfect contentment—that love is conditional.

All of us got to this state because our parents did what parents do: they domesticated us. Yes, they did their best. They taught us their values, language, and culture. They also ingrained their fears, doubts, religion, prejudices, and addictions into the core of our consciousness. (By the way, we will call this collection of entities/emotions/conditions "detractors.")

With all of these detractors dragging us down over the years, by now most of us have become just like our parents in all their imperfections. And it doesn't stop there. Whether we have children now or intend to have children in the future, we will eventually become agents that help perpetuate the insanity. In our careers, families, business dealings, and relationships, we do and will perpetuate the insanity.

I do not mean to lay all the blame on our parents, of course. Our teachers did not teach us well. They taught that our intuition is not dependable. They taught that we must accept ideal standards of control in order to be safe and that we must behave in a certain way if we hope to earn a reward. At almost no point during our schooling and upbringing did they allow us to be intuitive and spontaneous. And we rarely experienced unconditional love. They did not actively teach us to put an end to conflict, struggle, and resistance. Rather, they taught us to believe in the illusions of competition that they themselves treasured as pure truth.

From the time we could first understand words and direction, parents and teachers innocently began their never-ending task of convincing us that we are not perfect. As early as the age of three, we had completely forgotten the bliss of our previous existence. We had already become one of the disconnected people of this "natural" world. We no longer could practice unconditional love, mostly because every attempt to do so was met with a stern, bleak lesson.

Later on in our lives, other teachers, siblings, and friends joined the chorus that would rob us of our perfection. Collectively, our teacher's and peer group's favorite word was no. Through this constant cacophony of things we were not supposed to do, we slowly learned that we were not perfect. With this realization, our core beliefs and self-image became twisted and deformed into an insane pattern of cultural conformity accompanied by the detractors. We learned to assume the role of son or daughter, student, friend, brother or sister, lover, spouse, and father or mother. And the consequence of these relationships is always dictated by love based on some condition.

The overarching lesson is "Everything is conditional. Every act of love comes with a price. And love means control." In other words, we slowly learned that "I love you" also means "I control you." Through this harsh lesson, we came to realize (incorrectly and inconsistently) that it is good to gain comfort and avoid pain (at any cost); to gain attention and escape being ignored; to gain approval and escape rejection; to gain importance and escape feeling inferior. These values were molded into our consciousness and continue even into adulthood to control our thoughts, actions, ambitions, and relationships. On the world stage, these erroneous values, now ingrained in our collective consciousness, have created all the chaos that exists on the planet.

The true self-destruction—the true exodus from perfection—begins when we start seeking validation for our position in respect to everything we learned from the people and culture that raised us. It does not matter who we are; eventually, there comes a time when we seek validation in everything we do. Through all the negativity that surrounds us, we find ourselves needing to know that we are acknowledged, respected, and heard, not marginalized or dismissed. When we check ourselves in the mirror each day, we validate that we are ready to face the world by comparing our appearance to the sum of a culturally constructed understanding of what looks "good" or "acceptable." When we ask an opinion of another, we are seeking not their answer but rather their validation. In these ways, we always seek personal validation from someone other than ourselves.

It is no secret why so many of us have become driven by this hollow kind of validation, for receiving acknowledgment and validation from others can be an incredible rush. It feels like genuine respect and always provides a sense of security and belonging. It keeps us from feeling worthless or dismissed as immature or even crazy. In the extreme, needing validation from external sources (culture) often results in fanatical belief systems with the potential to sustain conflict between individuals, groups, religions, and countries.

Now think about the contrary ethos. If we do not receive validation, we feel as if we are not respected or socially accepted. This makes us feel uncomfortable, defeated, and sometimes worthless. This discomfort is so motivating that it becomes the primary driver of our behaviors, attitudes, worldview, and, most of all, unhappiness. We might have been born perfect, but through our need for validation, we have become slaves and victims.

Over the years, we became all of these things based on negative lessons. We were no longer who we really are. Rather, we became a fabrication, a false persona. As we grew, the suggestions that formed this false persona stayed and grew with us, becoming quite powerful in the process. Our egocentric focus became the overwhelming force in our lives.

This ego-based perspective has created a species of humans divided by race, religion, culture, language, and values—a veritable hell on earth. We were taught all of these things and shaped in this egocentric way in an effort to keep us safe and happy (whatever that might mean in such a state). The result is a personality based on a false understanding of who we are and how we align with the rest of the world. We are not happy. We are stressed. We are overwhelmed. We are unfulfilled. We are afraid. Through our false personalities and inflated egos, we have not found happiness; rather, we have created a world of sustained chaos.

How did this all come to pass? Are not all human beings desirous of joy and perfection? Of course we are. We are simply operating from a fundamental misunderstanding of our role in the universe, and that misunderstanding stems from our collective mismanagement of our most tremendous (and dangerous) gift: self-awareness. In the known world, we are the only life form that is self-aware. And yet, curiously, all other life forms seem better adjusted to their world than we are. As long as they are nourished, find safety, and have the opportunity to reproduce, they are content with almost anything that goes on around them. Don't believe me? Just watch a cat for a while and try to imagine what goes on in that little mind. If it is not eating, cleaning itself, or chasing something (whether for a meal or just for the fun of it), it does nothing more than relax. How wonderful does that sound?

Before we continue, let's consider a little exercise. With your grand self-awareness, compare the life and concerns of a cat to what goes on in your mind. May I suggest that you are not as happy and content as that little cat? Why do you suppose that is?

Your first instinct will be to say that it is because you have more responsibilities or obligations. You have a job, mouths to feed, bills to pay, etc. But these things are all incidental when compared to your ultimate contentment. No, you are unhappy compared to the cat because you have been wounded every day of your life. Throughout your upbringing, negativity has dominated your sensory input. You fell into the human trap of believing all this negative stuff is the truth. Your self-talk—the thoughts in your mind based almost solely on a lifetime of learning what you cannot or should not do—now rules your days and nights. Even when you do not realize you are doing it, you are turning this negative self-talk (detractors) in your mind over and over, day after day. You know what the troubling part is? This negative self-talk stems from a fundamental misunderstanding of the universe. We have been taught our whole lives that we are imperfect and undeserving of contentment. Our whole lives we have believed a lie.

Just think about where all that negativity stems. It is all based on the belief system your family and peers have shaped for you since birth. It all comes from the environments we have created for ourselves. As a result, we spend countless hours each day just wounding ourselves with negative self-talk. And the worst part? All that negativity is based on falsehoods. Consider the top three falsehoods that plague us all each day:

1. We are not good enough.
2. We are separated from our creator and from one another.
3. We are not all equal.

Even on the surface, these falsehoods seem completely damaging. But consider what they do to our behavior as a result:

1. We fill our bodies with toxic chemicals.
2. We fail to achieve self-validation.
3. We remain sedentary, allowing our bodies to turn to mush.
4. We fail to understand and practice unconditional love.
5. We fail to learn natural law.
6. We fail to align ourselves with the higher order of nature.

All of this wounding derives from erroneous conditioning that we have accepted as truth. Thinking that our success, indeed our very survival, depends on this body of actual falsehood, we have squandered our happiness. We perpetuate that falsehood by unconsciously wounding our loved ones and ourselves day after day, month after month, year after year—and even though we have no one but ourselves to blame for the insanity of our existence, we place that blame on someone or something other than ourselves. We blame our bosses. We blame our government. We blame the crime in our neighborhood. We blame the media. We blame our parents. We blame our spouses. We blame fate for dealing us a bad hand. Every day, we face our negative perceptions, and every day, we place ourselves on the throne of the victim. Every day, we judge. Every day, knowingly or unknowingly, we teach the next generation the same chaotic worldview.

Fortunately, this manner of living runs completely contrary to the natural way we can choose to live. If we want to find truth, peace, and happiness, we need only become aware of the natural way. Once we achieve that awareness, we can finally relax and enjoy our journey in this life. Make no mistake; it is never too late to enjoy the journey. And in this awareness, we can perceive our journey up until now as the perfect motivation to change our perspectives. We can now consciously and by choice return to our natural state of harmony, joy, and peace. We can live above the chaos.

Think about your life up to now. Would you say that it has been free of mistakes? Do you feel that there are people in your life who have wronged you? Do you feel that there is not one thing in your life that, if you could go back, you would do differently? How often do you think about these things?

Without even knowing it, you might think about them frequently. Sometimes we feel sorry for all the mistakes we have made. Sometimes we find ourselves in toxic relationships, boring jobs, poor health, and constant worry and conflict. But why should we feel this way? Soon you will appreciate that these discomforts serve a positive and definite purpose if you change your point of view. Soon you will appreciate that everything is perfect. There is, after all, no such thing as imperfection in this world. I am going to say this many time as we move along, but let me truly highlight it this first time:

> Everything is perfect. You are exactly the way Infinite Wisdom intended you to be. There is nothing else you need to know.

Think about that for a moment. You are perfect. You are exactly the way Infinite Wisdom has made you. There is nothing else that could ever be true. If we can know this, we also know that there is no such thing as a mistake. No one has ever wronged you. There is nothing in your life that you should have done differently or could have done better. Everything you are and everything you have done is a perfect reflection of what Infinite Wisdom presented to you as circumstances and choices required for your evolutionary journey. Infinite Wisdom creates nothing other than perfection. So if we can accept that we are the creation of Infinite Wisdom, we must also accept that we are perfect. And if we can accept that we are perfect, how could we possibly make mistakes?

No one feels this perfection or even understands it unless one becomes aware of certain natural laws. Then and only then can one perceive perfection in everyone and in everything; then and only then can one see that we are all perfect in every way, all the time.

Recall my point about how we all seek validation every day. When we do not receive it, it becomes the driver of many of our negative and chaotic behaviors. When we do receive it, we find ourselves contented, comfortable, and soothed by this warm sense of belonging. Every small measure of validation is an incredible feeling. So imagine for a moment what total self-validation would feel like. In other words, you would always feel the way you feel when other people validate your appearance, actions, or opinions—and that feeling would not be dependent on how other people view you. Rather, it would come from within. Every moment of every day, you would feel validated by yourself. Wouldn't that feel like freedom? Isn't that a state of being more in tune with who you want to be?

CHAPTER 2

CHANGING PERSPECTIVES

From this point forward, our aim will be to exercise our free will to evolve into an enlightened, or aware, state—to become the channel for the Universe to express here and now and the latest version of Infinite Wisdom's greatest vision. We will become more skilled and peaceful as we seek this enlightenment.

But this task seems so huge! Enlightenment seems so unattainable! This "seeming" is true, for what I ask you to start doing today is to take steps to evolve as a human being. We can initiate that process this very moment by our contemplation of the Metta Sutta of Buddhist teachings. The Metta Sutta establishes a mental picture of our true nature and gives us a context into which we may expand our awareness. Consider the Metta Sutta:

> May (we) be able and upright, straightforward, of gentle speech, and not proud. May all beings be happy. May they live in safety and in joy. All living beings, whether weak or strong, tall, stout, average or short, seen or unseen, near or distant, born or to be born, may they all be happy.

By now you may be wondering what qualifies me to speak to these compelling and life-changing topics. This is a good question. I am qualified in part because of my background as a physician/surgeon, but more than anything, I am qualified because I made the same evolution of consciousness that I intend to guide you through in this volume. It all began many years ago when suddenly I no longer felt like it made any sense to continue living in the chaos that we have collectively created in the world. I was creating and then destroying relationships and my health. And the chaos of my life was self-inflicted. As they say, doing the same thing over and over and expecting a different outcome is insanity. After three marriages and nine children, it became painfully obvious that although I was quick to blame others, I was the only common denominator, and I was addicted to chaos. Later, I will discuss the nature of chaos, but for now, consider chaos as any negative event that we attract or allow into our lives repeatedly.

When this realization hit me, I wanted to find a cave, crawl into it, and withdraw. But instead, I found myself on an airplane flying to Mexico, where, in Teotihuacan, I had a life-changing experience. My guide took me to the ancient pyramids located in a place "where man awakens to God." Really—that's what they call it. The Pyramid of the Sun is the largest and highest structure, and since I had an innate fear of heights, I initially planned to admire it from afar. But my guide had a different plan. We were going to climb to the very top, which on this cloudy day was barely visible. At that time, my fear of heights, dogs, and death was intense and unshakable. Reluctantly, I agreed to go halfway.

As I ascended the Pyramid of the Sun with my guide, I became frozen with fear. I reached the first level and could not move. I am not a coward, but there, halfway up the Pyramid of the Sun, I was immobilized.

"Tom," my guide said softly and in a manner that told me he was not surprised. "Look into my eyes and tell me what you see."

My breathing slowed and my fear subsided, as I saw a man radiating love and empathy. With the sun beating down on us and wispy clouds racing against the backdrop of the improbably blue sky, I saw what I now know as Christ consciousness. (This orientation was based on my cultural and religious background. One could just as easily have related to a Buddha consciousness or any philosophy based on love.) Yes, it was a peace that escaped my understanding. It was a feeling that told me I had nothing to fear. Nothing. For the first time in my life, I experienced and understood the power of unconditional love, for it radiated from this man.

"I feel compelled to jump off this pyramid," I told him. "But now I think I can fly like that eagle over there." Yes, amazingly, there was an eagle circling the pyramid. Bear in mind that the eagle in Native American culture is a sacred message from the Great Spirit—and here I witnessed the blessing of the sacred eagle circling the great Pyramid of the Sun, where man awakens to God.

"First we must reach the top," he said.

When I agreed, up we climbed. As we ascended further, I noticed that we had been joined by two other beings. Two ugly, seemingly diseased dogs began climbing the pyramid with us.

My phobia of dogs relates to experiences I had as a young boy. The paper route I managed required me to deliver papers to several homes guarded by vicious dogs. To earn my three dollars per week, I had to face this horror on a daily basis. Like most fears, this became a part of my very nature. My family knew that Tommie feared unfamiliar dogs. A fear of this nature can dominate our thinking and actions. Even as an adult jogging on the beach or in the neighborhood, I would go to any measure to avoid a confrontation with a dog—any dog. On this day at the pyramid, two dogs appeared at my side. Given our location, I could not escape. Even as I attempted to conquer one of my greatest fears, I found myself trapped with another.

But where before I would have feared these creatures, I now saw two gentle companions encouraging me to keep climbing. No fear, just gratitude. How does intense fear change to gratitude? What power do we possess when we change our perceptions from fear to unconditional love? Is it possible that I had learned a powerful lesson here? Maybe I didn't need to crawl into the cave of self-pity after all.

I do not consider this experience as a unique divine intervention. I was simply ready (receptive) to perceive and interpret everything as direct divine intervention. Everything. Given my depressed mental state at the time, I suppose I responded to a survival instinct that told me that if I did not change, my happiness and indeed my very survival were at risk.

The joy and excitement I felt as we continued the climb cannot be described. When we reached the top, my guide turned to me with a smile and said, "Tom, are you going to fly off this pyramid like the eagle?"

I smiled.

"You are just a man. You have not yet attained the wisdom of the eagle. And besides, you have no wings."

We had a good laugh.

Then very seriously, he added, "I am your brother. I brought you here.

If you jump off this pyramid, I must go with you."

I looked over the edge of the precipice, sweat dripping from my forehead and careening over the edge. There was a time that this would have made me feel weak in the knees. But that day was not one of those times. My spirit flew from the pyramid, but my body—along with my guide and my new canine friends—descended the pyramid on foot.

"Death does not matter to either one of us," he said on the way down. "For we are of infinity, we are eternal beings, and our only mission is to love."

From that moment, I understood the power of unconditional love. I understood that our only purpose is to feel love of self and to love everything. Our perceptions of negativity—as in our fears of things like heights and dogs—are only illusion. Our true nature is to love. Christ said it this way, "You are the light of the world." Until that moment atop the pyramid, I did not understand what those words truly meant. But there, I let go of my fear and accepted eternal and enduring love for all things. I evolved.

No other qualification to go on this journey exists except for an intention to evolve. Our source is Infinite Wisdom as expressed in the Universal Subconscious Mind.

The Universal Subconscious Mind

So what can we know about the Universal Subconscious Mind (USM)? We know that it has no beginning and no end, but is infinite and cannot adequately be characterized or defined in classical physical terms. And you know what is interesting about that statement? It also describes our true nature. Just like the Infinite Wisdom of USM, we have no beginning and no end. We are infinite and immortal. Those who understand this are truly rare on the planet. Those who actually believe it are even more rare. And once we identify such avatars, we usually destroy them in the name of some current cultural judgment. If we hope to learn the true nature of ourselves, we must first explore the true nature of the USM, God, Higher Power, the One, the Source, the Creator, or whatever other name you have for the infinite power that created us all and holds us all together. I choose to call that power the Infinite Wisdom of the USM, for I feel it best reflects both the infinite nature of life and the incredible reality that everything is perfect and as it should be. The energy field behind creation is indelibly wise. How could it be then that anything less than perfection exists? How could it be that your natural self is anything but perfect truth?

Your natural self, break it down. It starts with light, the energy that permeates all. The light physically manifests by self-transformation into subatomic particles, to atoms from perfect combinations of electrons, to molecules by perfect combinations of atoms, to amino acids by perfect combinations of molecules, to proteins from perfect combinations of amino acids, to life from perfect combinations of proteins. Life is the perfect manifestation of this sequence. You are the latest version of this sequence. You are perfect.

So, what is your true nature? Your true nature is nothing less than the concrete manifestation of divine energy, the Godhead of Infinite Wisdom. It is this same Infinite Wisdom that creates and maintains the entire universe. It might be an overwhelming thought at first, but this is only one of the many truths you will come to accept as you achieve a higher level of awareness. We are in fact no greater and certainly no less than the entirety of the universe.

Now, when I write a sentence like that, I know what I am up against. I know that, with your culture and upbringing, your first thought is going to be to resist that notion—at least until you can see some scientific evidence that substantiates even a shred of truth here. Obviously, I am going to need many pages of evidence to support the notion that you are no greater and no less than the entirety of the universe, coupled with the idea that your natural state is in fact one of perfection. But for now, let us consider that even the scientific community cannot counter the evidence that is available based on life experience.

Science, for example, cannot prove, disprove, or even explain the established fact of reincarnation. Accounts from dependable sources have documented numerous cases of individuals (especially young children) possessing knowledge that was available only in previous life situations. Let's think about this one small notion to get us started.

If you believe in reincarnation and base this belief on accounts presented by reputable reports and documented cases, what exactly is the mechanism for reincarnation? Science tells us that the entire universe is permeated by an energy force and that this force of energy can be measured and manipulated. Light energy for example, becomes matter and matter can become light energy.

Still you doubt? Let's examine some additional information that is not explainable using conventional physics. In his brilliant book God Is Not Dead, Amit Goswami, PhD, examines scientific evidence that convincingly proves the existence of an Agent of Causation (the agent here termed the Universal Subconscious Mind). Goswami's "God hypothesis" is based on the concept of quantum nonlocality, or signal-less communication. Extensive laboratory experiments dating as far back as 1982 demonstrate that information can be transmitted instantly without regard to distance or location. The concept of the

USM essentially explains this process and was first explored in 1954 by U. S. Anderson in his book Three Magic Words.

What, exactly, does this prove? Well, even to the skeptical scientific community, these and other laboratory findings indicate that energy forces indeed pervade the universe. The USM is the repository of this wisdom and permeates all existence. These forces do not adhere to our classic understanding of reality or even to classical physics. It proves that there is a field of energy, a force, a power that transcends any previous understanding. Call it what you may, we will discuss how this power is the Infinite Wisdom of the USM.

So we know scientific pursuits (as well as our life experience) provide indisputable evidence for the existence of phenomenon we recognize as reincarnation and signal-less communication. Is this in fact God? Does it mean there is no father figure in long white robes and a long white beard; no vengeful old man hanging out at the golden gates of heaven waiting to judge you?

Even members of the scientific community can buy into this concept now. If you can accept that understanding, the next step is to accept that you are a reflection of that energy field. Even though the Bible teaches that heaven is found within, acceptance is difficult, I know. The false persona you have grown and shaped over the years has assured your physical survival and even a role in society. But at the same time, that false persona has temporarily separated your intellect from the Source, Infinite Wisdom, and your perfect self. Whether you accept the principles of this book or not, know this for certain: over the course of your life, you will learn many things that will help you to find your way back. No matter what you think today or what you do tomorrow, you will be back. This is our ultimate destiny. Just as all water eventually returns to the oceans, our true nature eventually returns to its Source. As water flows, we evolve.

What else can we know about the USM? We know that it is changeless. We might perceive change in our lives and in our world, but the Creator and Source for everything does not change. This means that change is illusion. Our material world is pure illusion. Our physical bodies are illusion. Our perceived condition of not being enough or not having enough is also illusion. The USM, being infinite and wise in every conceivable (and inconceivable) way, is omnipotent, omni-present, and omni-everything. We might find ourselves placed here in this physical world with no recollection of our previous perfection, but because our Source is perfection, we, too, are perfection—whether we know and accept this or not.

I believe that everything is perfect. All perceived imperfections are illusions. All negative thought is a result of my domestication. I am alive and healthy, and I believe I always have been. My survival is never threatened because I belong to infinity. I believe that as a being of infinity, I am not restricted to the narrow perceptions of sight, smell, sound,

taste, or touch. I believe that I have the powers of imagination and intuition to create my life as the latest version of God's greatest vision. I can serve others by sharing this vision of perfection. I accomplish this by banishing all doubt and negative thinking. I can love uncon-ditionally, recognizing that everyone does the best that he or she can within his or her personal level of awareness. I believe that through the practice of unconditional love, I can forgive any transgression. I believe in the connective nature of all life forms as one integrated consciousness that emanates from Infinite Wisdom. I do not subject myself to the concepts of pain, disease, shame, guilt, apathy, grief, fear, or anger. I can imagine into existence peace, joy, love, reason, acceptance, and courage. I believe the world will evolve by rediscover-ing natural law.

The illusions of insanity and chaos in this world were important tools in the ascent of my personal journey into awareness. The insan-ity and chaos you have experienced will serve you as well.

Today, I feel gratitude for all things, and I accept all things as per-fect. After all, Infinite Wisdom is perfection. Living and thinking in this way is the greatest joy and peace that a human being can experi-ence. Making this transformation utterly changed my life for the bet-ter. I wish the same experience for you because I believe together we shall enhance the evolution of our species and our children will learn by our example. This is the way to a joyful and peaceful life. Moreover, this is the only path to world peace.

Exploring a New Approach

If understood and followed, natural law can put an end to the illusion of suffering. We must keep and respect the law, and in our modern environment, this is not an easy task. Fortunately, there is a grand secret that will absolutely change our perspective on the matter: surrender. Unless we accept a new awareness and attain higher insight, complete surrender is nearly impossible. Yet surrender can be an easy task for those who are ready. Ready means receptive, remember? Our life experience ensures our readiness. If you have ever experienced any degree of suffering, you are ready. If you are tired of suffering, you are receptive.

Once you are aware of the natural law and commit to live by it, you will not want to live by any other standard. It will feel so right, peaceful, and natural that you will never want to return to your previous state of chaos. This natural law is really the very set of energies that has sustained you from the beginning. And by "the beginning" I mean the very beginning, back to that era when the very forms that created you were first assembled.

Now think about this: before our present form (that is, our life on earth), everything required for our physical needs was provided for and created in perfection. From the moment of our physical conception, we were sustained, protected, nourished, and guided perfectly in the womb. We didn't consciously ask for nor did we have any control over this process, yet here we are. Our best interests in this physical life form were assured. Then, nine months later, we entered the world. We entered with the kind of infinite potential that one might compare to a computer with a perfectly programmable hard drive.

Yes, we may be thinking at this point about how challenging and downright difficult our lives have been. We have struggled, been abused, and have abused. We have tried and failed. Our lives have not been the perfect, romantic, "happily ever after" story. The software loaded into our perfect computer has become defective. These things are true and undeniable. But take solace, for natural law states that everything we have ever experienced, witnessed, learned, or felt was perfectly arranged to get us to this very moment, this very place of perfect motivation to become aware of this next concept. Make no mistake. You are ready for this concept. How do I know you are ready? I believe beyond any doubt that you would never have read the preceding ideas without a good reason. Your reason is your intention, and your intention is your desire. You possess an innate desire to evolve. Life always evolves; you are of infinity, so there is no death. You are an eternal energy being. You will continue to evolve no matter what you think or do. The amazing awareness is that you can direct your evolution by your intention.

You are ready!

Here is the law you have been waiting to discover all these years, the natural law that you must understand and make a central theme in your belief system as you evolve. This is the one natural law that allows everything to happen:

> Surrender your will, your power, your plans, your talents,
> and your control to the Infinite Wisdom of the USM.

The natural law is to surrender to the power that created you and connects all life into infinity. When you think about it, what other intelligent choice is there? The more we contemplate this concept, the more it actually resonates with our true nature. We started life in surrender, after all, and we will end it in surrender as well. Knowing this truth, we must also know that it is true that we will benefit if we make a conscious intention to surrender now, at this very moment. Why wait? Why wait until we are on our deathbed? Why wait when it is entirely possible to achieve that same deathbed enlightenment now while we still have all this time to live on this playground, we call planet Earth?

The concept of surrender may conjure up for you an uncomfortable feeling of defeat or weakness. If so, you are not yet aware of how and why one surrenders to Infinite Wisdom. Consider that in the worldly parameters of surrender, there may indeed be a winner and a loser. Someone may surrender his possessions, territory, or ideals to another who perhaps "won the battle" and proclaims himself the victor. But in Infinite Wisdom, there is no conflict. There is no victor or judge, no selling, buying, or trading, and certainly no conflict. Surrender in the context of Infinite Wisdom is like the surrender we experienced when two strands of DNA joined together to create a new individual. It requires nothing of us except a conscious intent. Infinite Wisdom in that context is the cause of every effect. This entity knows only unconditional love and unlimited abundance. All human affairs, having been created by humans, mean nothing to Infinite Wisdom. We are like two little kids fighting over the same toy when the entire room is full of toys, with one even better than the next.

Surrendering means to submit to the flow of the positive powers of the USM. If this flow is compared to the current of a river, it means we give up the idea of moving against that current. We should do this as soon as possible because fighting against the evolutionary and everexpanding flow of the universe is needlessly wasting our energy. Going with the flow is the path to becoming more authentic. Authenticity gives us power. This authentic power is power over our selves.

The first step in surrendering is to surrender your ego. Man created the ego as a tool to establish self-worth, but our self-worth cannot be established by our comings, goings, learning, doing, successes, or failures. Our worth is established and insured by Infinite Wisdom. "Nothing you do or think or wish or make is necessary to establish your worth" (A Course In Miracles, Helen Schucman).

We will talk in depth about the ego and how you let it go in the next chapter, but for now, concentrate on bringing ego back into balance with your imagination. Those things you perceive with your senses are not real. You make them real by your belief and conditioning. Consider, for example, that ancient peoples once observed the earth as a flat surface floating on a massive sea. It appeared that the sun revolved around the earth. This belief was so strong that theorizing otherwise was punished by death or imprisonment.

But through surrender, you can let go of your conditioned, uptight, stressed-out, controlling, sick, maladjusted, and egocentric self. The result is a new, relaxed, accepting, healthy, integrated, serving self, a self-revived to live in love, peace, and joy. The best part about this surrender is that, contrary to the helpless images the word might conjure in your mind, it is the ultimate form of self-control. When you have surrendered to Infinite Wisdom, you gain the power to decide what you want, act upon your intent, do your best, and then let go, or detach. It is akin to letting yourself rest in the hands of God, allowing His power to lovingly and effortlessly carry you through your existence.

Eventually, we all will get this concept, even if we wait until our death, because death is the ultimate surrender of ego, and at that point, we have no choice.

When you attempt to surrender, one of two things will happen. Either your beautiful life will automatically appear in an effortless way or it won't. If the latter is what manifests for you, do not fret. It does not mean that you are somehow incapable of accepting natural law. It means only that Infinite Wisdom has a better plan for you. It means you have not yet endured enough suffering to tip your motivational drive in favor of full surrender. Consider briefly here that everything is as it should be. You may be very reasonable in questioning this concept, but for now, attempt to go with this intuitive feeling based on your own desire to evolve.

Surrender does not mean giving up. The only way to surrender is to focus your energy away from suffering and accept that Infinite Wisdom is guiding you toward the ultimate goal in a way that perfectly suits you.

As we contemplate natural law, we enter a higher level of awareness by understanding why complete surrender makes so much sense.

The following list should assist you in your understanding of these new concepts:

1. We have already experienced surrender once—on the day we received the gift of life.

2. We really don't know what is good for us. The Creator (Infinite Wisdom) of all things creates only what is good for us. Through natural law (unconditional love and evolution), the Creator has always made our best interests a priority.

3. At the moment of death, we surrender our egocentric self. This is natural law. No "body" makes it out alive.

4. We have been given the gift and abilities for deliberate creation. We choose (from infinite possibilities through imagination) what we want and how we want to live. Nothing happens unless we make it so. And we make it so first in consciousness (imagination).

5. We try to manage and control our lives, but we do so with limited knowledge. We can't make the ultimate best choices because we don't have all the facts.

6. Infinite Wisdom is outside of any human concept of the Creator and therefore is not a part of any philosophy. All human concepts (philosophies) are folly when viewed from the eternal nature of Infinity.

Consider this example. Before you start out on a road trip, you get your map ready and get the best advice for your route. You set your GPS to your desired destination. Since you have gathered all the information you need, you can see that you must proceed in a certain direction down a certain pathway and turn left for the best and most direct route. You have all the facts, have made good preparation, and are on your way to taking the best route.

But wait! A flash flood has just washed out the road. Turning left was a big mistake. The road is gone. You are now caught in the flood and are carried downstream to an uncertain destination and fate.

How did this happen? You did everything right. You researched the best route to accomplish your goal, and you thought you had all the facts you needed. This happened because you were wrong about the notion that you had all the facts. You knew everything there was to know about the ideal route, but you could not possibly have anticipated the flood. You made a terrible mistake in thinking you had it all right. And the result? You are carried downstream to an unpredictable fate and an unknown destination.

This metaphor describes our feeble attempts at controlling our lives. It often seems like bad things happen to us for no reason, but that is merely because we don't really know all the facts (even when we think we do). So we blunder our way through life, trying this, trying that, making bad turns, and getting into trouble. We fail, we react, we think we can control, we stress, and we become disenchanted, discouraged, and ultimately sick.

Is there a better way? Well, yes, there is. Surrender. Give your control to Infinite Wisdom. Infinite Wisdom not only has all the facts but also controls all the natural forces that cause the facts to be known. Once we are aware of natural law, we enter a world of perceiving Infinite Wisdom as a force that is on our side. We know that our best interests are always served. It cannot be otherwise and it has always been.

So how does this work in our daily personal lives? Do we just sit around saying, "Okay, I surrender. Help me!" No, not even close. In the chapters to come, I will help you reach a deeper understanding of this concept of surrender. Then I will guide you through the steps toward the highest possible level of awareness. But for now, keep in mind that these are the general steps toward a deeper understanding and acceptance of natural law: follow your heart; follow your intuition; decide what you want, where you want to be, and who you want to be with; using your imagination, set an intention and then move in that direction; and take some action, work at it, and then surrender and detach from the outcome, knowing that by thinking positive thoughts, the outcome will ultimately be established.

By following these steps, we can have a relaxed and beautiful life, no matter what happens. We can be a vessel for creation, love, energy, and the perfection of Infinite Wisdom.

There was once a wise man named Paul. His accomplishments were quite impressive. While in prison, he wrote some letters to his friends, letters of love and encouragement. Many years later, these letters were translated and compiled into the most widely read manuscript on the planet. The book, although it has undergone many revisions, became the basis of an entire religion. This book is the New Testament of the Bible. The man was Saint Paul.

In effect, Saint Paul said that we should not worry about anything, that we should ask God (Infinite Wisdom) for what we need. He said that God's peace will keep our hearts and minds safe. He said that we should fix our thoughts on what is true, and honorable, and right, and pure, and lovely, and admirable. That sounds an awful lot like surrender to natural law.

In reality, what are we to surrender? We are to surrender our thoughts, for it is they that create our ultimate destiny.

Every one of us has an inner monologue going on inside our heads. If we hope to evolve toward surrender, it is necessary that we pay close attention to this inner monologue constantly churning and creating our reality. We banish this negative monologue by replacing it with positive affirmations. We can by an act of will enter the surrendering state of mind by banishing negative thoughts. If that inner voice speaks of negative entities, the ultimate result will reflect these thoughts. We can control this churning by being aware of its significance. As we think, so shall we be. It's a self-fulfilling prophecy. This awareness of our inner monologue determines our sense of being. It is a familiar yet intangible miracle. Surrendering takes the power of this inner monologue and converts it from a negative attractor force to a positive one.

Later in this volume, we will explore the exact psychological and scientific explanations for this power we possess to attract positive outcomes. You may be surprised at the power you have over all the

physical and nonphysical aspects of your life. You have in fact knowingly or unknowingly created yourself and your environment first in
your imagination.

As your awareness increases, you will understand that your subconscious mind (as a direct link to Infinite Wisdom) creates for you
exactly what your conscious mind has accepted into your belief system as true. This is the reason we come to know there is nothing
to worry about. The awareness of the powerful relationship we can
cultivate with Infinite Wisdom through our thinking represents the
specific knowledge we need to ultimately surrender and live above
the chaos.

We Are the Sons and Daughters of the Sun

It's true. We are the sons and daughters of the sun. A belief in this concept is vital to understanding why we are the latest version of God's
greatest vision. The story goes as follows:

First, there was the Intelligence (Infinite Wisdom). Nothing exists
or has ever existed outside of this Intelligence. Nothing predates it.
This Intelligence is the law. There is nothing extraneous to the law.
The law is pure energy. Pure energy became manifest into pure light,
or vibrational energy. This light evolved into a particle that represented the first of our physical form. The particle then became two,
and by natural Intelligence, they attracted each other. Thus, an atom
was formed by the attraction of Intelligence, one to the other. The law
of attraction now called gravity brought all matter together into a tiny
spot. Then the big bang occurred. The known cosmos was created
from this one moment of unity.

Eventually, the cosmos included our sun and its surrounding
solar system. All things on Earth originated from this location. All
life on Earth originates from the relationship between the sun and
Earth. The sun is our father; the earth is our mother. We are sons
and daughters of the sun. And we are all related by our common
Source.

We Are the Sacred Temples

The creation event establishes the incredible relationship of all physical matter, including life forms. A belief in the above point about our source of the sun would naturally lead one to an important conclusion: not only are we all related due to our Source, but we are all also sacred temples, manifestations of the divine energy that created everything. The real self is not the body but the infinite energy that is Infinite Wisdom. Put another way, we are all one. And that oneness includes all the energy there is, even into Infinity.

Our physical bodies are divine energy manifested as matter. Innately, the energy of our physical bodies originates and is a part of Infinite Wisdom. That energy naturally reflects its Source. We acknowledge the sacred fire of love. We care for it and venerate it. It is life. We love life. This is the way of the natural law.

Once you have achieved a belief in all this, you will experience your body and your place here quite differently. Love to you will become sacred fire energy, an energy that you will want to share, as it has been given to you by the Source. You did not create it, earn it, or take it; it is the innate nature of everything. If we are aware of these relationships, we start to feel better. Under this belief, after all, everything is perfect. What more could we ever want?

The Challenge of Change

As we move forward through this journey together, let us choose to take an optimistic approach. There is a different way of seeing the world. We can see life as a great party put on by a magnificent Host. In many ways, we have this ability as a birthright. Yet only those who have an interest and initiative to study into awareness can benefit by this uncommon perspective. This awareness is open and available to anyone, yet it is our life journey that prepares and shapes our willingness to evolve.

You must make a conscious decision to change. This decision is the first crucial step. And then you must see in your reality what exactly you want to change and must believe it is possible to change. You must first want to change, identify what you will change, and then believe you can change.

This book will serve to facilitate a change in your perception that could possibly elevate your level of awareness. And if your level of awareness increases and your perception changes, maybe you can start feeling better. There is no reason why you should not start feeling better. Feeling better advances your purpose. Happy people influence others to be happy. Unhappy people create chaos. Feeling better is exactly what the world needs right now.

As we embark upon this journey, we will not see visions or hear voices. We do not write with a magic spirit pen or develop mystical meditation skills. No entity visits our house or sits on our shoulders. Our miracle comes from within by a natural process of awareness and a realization that even one breath of air, one heartbeat, and one life is a miracle.

Our main motivation is experience and an acquired sense of purpose. The wisdom required is already there, waiting to be rediscovered. It is that life experience that serves us up the perfect motivation to pursue a rational and more grounded existence.

If we hope to do this, we must first embrace the concept that something must change. Change is one of the few things in our lives that we can know for certain will occur. The only thing constant is change. We may fight it, or we may embrace it. Embracing change means that we begin to appreciate it and, in essence, take advantage of it as an opportunity. The only thing expected in change is the unexpected: everything that was isn't and everything that isn't is coming.

If you embrace change, or even seek it out as a way to improve your life, it can represent a radical deconstruction of what is and a radical reconstruction of what you want. You have the power to direct the process of change.

Consider yourself at the crossroads. You are facing radical choices. You can choose to let change happen or you can choose to make it happen. Letting change happen is a matter of giving up our power to external forces and circumstances. Making change happen is a matter of taking responsibility for our lives and gifting ourselves with self-validation.

Change does not lead to catastrophe. We can indeed go boldly forward, even if we don't know the exact outcome or destination. We can shake the foundation of our existence and create a new reality. We are emerging from our era of darkness into the light of a new dimension. We are the creator of our fondest intentions. We accomplish this by observing and living by natural law. We are sons and daughters of the sun. We are the sacred temples. We are one single entity. Our energy is the fire of love, which reflects the greater light of Infinite Wisdom. This is the way of the natural law.

As you embark on this quest, consider that the entire universe is alive and conscious. Even the minute subatomic particles and the vibrational energies adhere to natural law; therefore, all of existence evolves toward success, love, health, peace, and a grand purpose.

I look forward to embarking upon this journey with you, my friend. I look forward to change. I look forward to helping you return to your natural state, helping you to become the latest version of God's greatest vision. I look forward to helping you arrive at your optimal life. Let's begin.

We are one thing because of our Source. If we love ourselves, we can love all things. If we love all things, all races, all peoples, there is peace.

CHAPTER 3

The Case for Ego

The Dalai Lama has said that although it is possible to achieve happiness, happiness is not a simple thing. According to Buddhist teachings, there are many levels of happiness. I have chosen to mention the following four areas of happiness here:

1. Wealth
2. Worldly satisfaction
3. Spirituality
4. Enlightenment

Wealth and worldly satisfaction seem to go together, as does spirituality and enlightenment. Everyone has his or her own perspective on what these concepts mean. Of course, one may have massive wealth and still be unhappy if it doesn't create worldly satisfaction. Just observe wealthy people. My experience tells me that most (not all) are unhappy and they cause a disproportionate amount of trouble.

So, we see that happiness is not a given, but seeking happiness can often feel like looking for the pot of gold at the end of the rainbow. The search may become so frustrating that we find unhappiness instead. Perhaps we are searching for happiness when we should just allow happiness to find us.

Most of humankind lives in quiet desperation, a zombie-like existence geared toward survival on the physical plane. Happiness in that arena can be found in a good meal or being able to cover the rent. It can be found in a stimulating, well-paid job; a great, enduring relationship; a solid, healthy body; and a sense of security. This kind of happiness is important (and maybe even essential), but it is transient and therefore cannot exist on the level of true reality. The truth is never-ending, and all enduring, and so truth can never change or even suffer unhappiness.

Awareness of these concepts can help us experience happiness without searching for happiness. Yes, going from unhappy to happy can be a challenge, but it is well worth the effort. One way to go about it is to achieve a new level of awareness and appreciation for our earthly experience. We are here in this place for a brief opportunity to realize the physical while sensing the influence of the spiritual (often described as our outer world and our inner world). Interestingly, we know from realworld experience that the latter can influence the former.

We are going to investigate some of these findings in chapter 4. There is, after all, a convincing body of evidence that demonstrates that consciousness precedes matter—or in other words, that a thought or idea (spirit) determines outcome (our physical reality). Yes, we can become aware that the spiritual (mental) realm can influence the physical realm, but before we can get into a discussion of how and why that is so, we must first discuss what is preventing us from achieving the power and awareness to create our reality through our mental faculties and spirituality. In a nutshell, it is the ego (our own damaging vanity) that keeps us imprisoned in the physical realm and limits our potential for happiness.

With this chapter, I intend to first dispel some of the misconceptions about the ego before moving into a study on how we can rebalance its influence on our lives, thereby freeing ourselves to accept natural law, achieve a higher level of awareness, and move closer to becoming the perfect beings we were created to be.

There are a lot of negative ideas concerning the ego. This seems strange. If everything is perfect (having been created by Infinite Wisdom), how could we possibly look at the ego in a negative light? Well, it starts with our lack of understanding on the subject. Our level of awareness of the true purpose for the ego is and always has been quite low. Some say that the ego is responsible for all the greed, avarice, selfishness, division, hate, fear, war, and suffering in the world. This may be true when the natural law of balance within the ego is broken, but balance in nature is perfection, and suffering is nothing more than nature's perfect tool for restoring balance.

The ego does not create suffering unless the imbalance in its favor is tipped to the ultimate extreme: egomania. Egomania is the insane preoccupation with self at the expense of others and at the exclusion of an awareness of our true nature. In a sense, egomania is the opposite of ultimate awareness.

But I am getting ahead of myself here. First, we need to talk about what I mean when I write "balance." Balance means that we are aware of the perfection of all things. Acceptance of this concept dictates our surrender to Infinite Wisdom's perfect plan for mankind. That plan has resulted in an evolutionary process that has, over millions of years of earth time, resulted in a diverse and remarkable planet filled with beauty and abundance. The ego of our own species has been the driving force that allowed this perfect evolutionary process to unfold. And now that we have evolved to our present state, our awareness of these relationships dictates that we balance our egomania against our true nature, which is the eternal state of spirit. I contend that the eternal state of spirit is in fact pure unconditional love liberated from the constraints of ego.

Notice that I keep using the word balance. This is because we are not looking to banish the ego from our minds. It does, after all, serve great purpose. What we are attempting to do here is find a new role for the ego, a new level of contribution to our lives. The ego, after all, has always had its purpose. It was and is a positive force that assures our survival as the unstoppable force of evolution drives us into higher levels of awareness.

Yes, the ego is absolutely essential. We have not given it enough credit for assuring our survival in the world of form. Our egocentric orientation of separation has created a world based on survival of the fittest, competition, striving for superiority, and all of our baser instincts. The ego has seen us through thousands of years of physical survival to the present. Without it, we would not be where we are today.

That statement can be taken as a good or bad thing, though, right? There are many positive things about this physical realm we have created for ourselves, but there are many negative things as well. This is because, though the ego is quite a useful tool, we have always wielded it too heavily. It is human nature to overemphasize the ego force and underemphasize the spiritual force. This has created plenty of physical advancement but also plenty of chaos. The ego has its uses, but until now, we have relied entirely too much on those uses. Now it is time to rein in our egocentric propensities and remember our spiritual origins.

How do we know if have been unbalanced in our ego-based relationships? Egomania means we always have to be right. We are blind to another point of view. We fail to see another perspective. We cannot admit to ourselves that we are suffering or causing suffering. We can be blinded by egomania. We can allow the detractors of negativity, anger, and hatred to control our lives. We can justify these concepts by failing to control our own sensibilities.

But being one with Infinite Wisdom, we may sense the significance of another natural law: we must use our time in this life for enjoyment and following our desires while helping others do the same. This is our ego strength defined in a positive way: pursue delight, allow riches, and radiate joy. Our strong egos defined in this way give us a sense of purpose.

Our egos could and should create positive feelings of strength in others and ourselves. This is the positive, natural side of the ego: achievement and service.

The Analogy of the Birds

Two birds come into your life, one black and the other white. The raven rules the roost. He always reminds you of how important your five senses are. If you can see it, taste it, hear it, touch it, or smell it, according to the raven, it is real. In this way, your pain is real and comes in many forms. It matters not to the raven. He knows that he controls your thoughts all the time. He even shows up in your dreams.

On the other hand is a white dove. She hangs back, for she is shy. But she knows that eventually she will come to rule the day. The raven cannot endure forever. His hold over you will surely fade as you take your last breath and the illusion of realness departs. The raven after all represents the ever-changing world of form while the dove is everlasting truth. What remains in death? What good are your five senses and what is real then? The raven represents the world of physical manifestation (illusion) while the dove represents the truth of Infinity. Physical manifestation is illusion because it constantly changes (the raven). Truth is infinite and unchanging (the dove).

You see, this higher level of truth in the form of the white dove is an enduring reality that cannot change. Even at physical death, the dove prevails. Even before death, the dove can intervene upon request and belief. The dove is pure, unconditional love.

The birds represent exactly the kind of duality of the mind that we're talking about in this chapter. They represent thoughts and ideas, one based on the world of form, the other based on desire and imagination. The birds can coexist, but one must always rule. Most likely, the raven represents your present situation. He is your concept of your life. He is your answer when you are asked to define yourself. And how do you define yourself? Are you your income, physical appearance, race, and all your problems? The white dove, meanwhile, defines how you want these answers to be, not what they are. In summary, the birds represent who you are compared to who you want to be.

Put another way, the raven is the problem and the white dove is the answer to the problem. The raven thrives on egomania while the only force that relates to the dove is unconditional love. We have control over our conscious thoughts. We can symbolically bleed the raven to death by taking away its strength, which lies only in our thoughts. And turning our attention away from our problems is the same as extracting the blood from the bird. We cannot expect great things to happen if we dwell on the past or become obsessed with our perceived problem. The blood, our consciousness, is what controls all of reality. Our conscious awareness of this will make a huge difference in our lives. So turn your attention to the white dove (unconditional love). She will carry your desires to fruition: illness to health, conflict to resolution, poverty to wealth, and stress to peace.

The Challenge of Perfection

As you make this journey, remember that everything is perfect. This may be a difficult concept to appreciate. I mean, we have so many problems in this life. We are not always happy and "bad" things can happen even to "good" people. So how can we perceive perfection in this? I can only speak for myself now, but at one point, I realized that there were two possibilities: either life is not perfect as a whole or I was missing something. As it turns out, I was missing something very obvious. It's that I was so busy being miserable that I really didn't think independently. I was part of the miserable herd so I could comfortably share my misery with everyone around me.

Well, I eventually decided that miserable people make everyone they encounter miserable. I wish someone had told me to shut up and count my blessings a whole lot earlier in my life. I admit that it was my daughter who one day said, "Dad, I love you, but shut up and count your blessings."

So now I am telling you to shut up and count your blessings. Everything is perfect. Our Source is perfection, and that makes everything perfect.

But how can we really believe that and still function in this world that seems so messed up? You might have suspected that I am eventually going somewhere with this thought. Okay, here it is: the belief that everything is perfect can be rendered from the teachings of all the avatars and savants. In essence, even Christ said to be thankful in all things. If he said, "all things," well, that surely meant all things. Everything is perfect.

Think back to that analogy of the birds. Symbolically we enter this world accompanied by the raven and the white dove. They, like us, are tiny, perfect little chicks. But they carry the knowledge and power and wisdom of the universe. The raven is dominant. He always reminds us that our new life in form now depends on our five senses. If we see it, taste it, hear it, feel it, or smell it, it exists. If we become uncomfortable, we are to seek comfort. We can survive this ordeal by conforming to the culture into which we have landed. So, by conforming and learning how to survive in the world of form, we acquire the same characteristics as our parents, teachers, and peer groups.

The white dove is also with us. She is shy but senses her power and indeed her permanence. She knows that the raven's orientation into the illusion of form cannot endure. She knows that the raven tells us how we are while the white dove tells us how we want to be. The raven represents conformity and cultural conditioning while the white dove represents thinking from the Source (Infinite Wisdom).

Fortunately, most people eventually evolve into beings that adhere more to the influences of the dove than the raven. The transformation is usually as follows:

1. Early in our lives, the raven serves us well by influencing us to learn about the physical world. We learn about competition, scarcity, and failure—as well as the good stuff, like winning, abundance, and success. We learn to judge and to be a victim. We experience abuse and we abuse. We become egomaniacs. Our relationship with the white dove is minimal, if it exists at all. We have no time for such nonsense when we are young. So at this point, it's like the raven scores a ten while the white dove stands at zero.

2. As we experience life, we begin to question the raven's approach. It hurts too much, and we eventually get tired of repeating the same old negative behavior. Ah, but the white dove is wise and patient. She starts her predictable influence on a mind that is now perfectly motivated toward change. She stimulates our imagination. We begin to visualize a better way to live. We may turn to religion, read a self-help book, or attend a seminar. At this point, the score evens up, raven at five and white dove at five.

3. Time passes, and predictably, as our physical strength and sometimes our health wanes, we spend more thought energy with the white dove. She understands. We encounter books, programs, or people who now begin to make sense. We have less and less time and energy for physical pursuits. Now it's raven three and white dove seven.

4. By the time of death, when we have accepted all that is true above all that we perceive with our five senses, the score has reversed completely. Raven zero, white dove ten.

In this life, some never leave that first phase. They spend their entire lifespan in hot pursuit of something without ever really knowing what that something is. For the rest of us, our discomfort provides the perfect motivation to evolve. Everything really is perfect, even when it doesn't seem to be. Having a desire for change is the perfect use of our imagination. This awakens the white dove. As life progresses, at some point we strike the perfect balance between the raven and the white dove. Life becomes good, a place where we can throw a party hosted by faith in our imagination. Toward the end, we feel better and better as we slide the scale in favor of the dove. Most of us are moving toward the dove, whether we realize it or not.

The choice is therefore ours. We can either wait and join her at death or we can use our imagination and balance our lives in the perfect way. The choice should be simple. After all, everything is perfect.

A Story ...

Before we move into an overview of how we will achieve this new balance, I would like to share a story about how I first came to many of the realizations that serve the premise of this book. After finally finishing my residency training in general surgery, my solo practice was about to begin. Achieving that goal was costly not only in financial terms but, more importantly, in terms of personal relationships and family. My divorce was something I couldn't imagine, and yet here I was in a second failing marriage, creating a broken home for six children.

I had no money, connections, or business experience. Luckily, I landed a job in an emergency room, a job that allowed me to at least feed and house my family.

I would not be long at this first hospital, however, because they denied my attempt at getting surgical privileges. This was in part because I literally walked out of the interview when one of the committee members asked me why I was divorced. I told her that it was none of her business. For a while, I wondered whether my ego would ever allow me to hold down a job at a place that would ask such a question. It turned out that it did not.

Just when it seemed like there would be nothing for me there, I secured a job at another nearby for-profit hospital, where they did indeed grant me surgical privileges despite my being divorced. The big question in the interview there was "Are you willing to take ER call and treat trauma victims?"

"Yes," I said. "Absolutely. I would be honored to do that." The next question was "Do you have malpractice insurance?"

Well, yes, I did—and for me, it was not too expensive because I was in my first year of practice when the premiums are still reasonable. This seemed like an odd line of questioning to me, but I discovered later that the established surgeons of the community were refusing to take ER call because there was a "malpractice crisis" in the area. Premiums were so expensive and the legal environment was so threatening that the informed and experienced surgeons could not (or would not) afford to take ER call.

For me, this crisis presented an opportunity. I was in complete denial as to the risks and commitment required to become a trauma surgeon in the region. (This was years before the concept of trauma centers became a reality, and it was a time when a general surgeon taking trauma call was basically flying solo.) No one wanted to get involved in these cases—especially not in a for-profit hospital—but I was fresh out of training, naïve as the day is long, and a pure disaster in the making.

Naturally, the other staff physicians welcomed me with open arms. Wow! I thought. What a great bunch of people to work with! Little did I know, they only appreciated me because I had agreed to do the one thing none of them would touch with a ten-foot pole. On my first day of trauma call, I learned that my colleagues were not as supportive as they had at first seemed. They would in fact go to any length to avoid becoming involved in trauma cases.

Not to worry. I pressed on, regardless. But this is not why I bring up this story. I bring it up because my first trauma case at my new hospital represented the dawn of my perception of Infinite Wisdom and the divine and graceful perfection of existence. Previous to this first case, I functioned as a senior and chief resident in surgery. I had always had a supportive team, plenty of back-up help, and mentors to call upon. But today, this first day of trauma call, I would be completely on my own— not only the captain of the ship but the entire crew as well. I remember both dreading and relishing that thought as I drove the unfamiliar route to my new office.

As I took the ramp onto the freeway, I received a page. I pulled over to a pay phone to call the hospital (no cell phones in 1984). It was the ER doc, and he was succinct: "Tom, we have a seventeen-year-old female with multiple injuries. The paramedics report no blood pressure, nonresponsive, and a grossly distended abdomen. They want to call it off. What say you?"

"What do you mean, they want to call it off?"

"They want to pronounce her dead, you know, DOA."

I looked to my watch to mark the time, feeling my heart start to race and my adrenaline surge. "I'm not going to do that. Get an IV going and continue life support protocol. Call in the OR crew for immediate surgery."

To this day, I have no idea why I responded that way. I mean, the situation was hopeless, wasn't it? My colleague had told me as much. Sure, I didn't know anything about him at that point, but he was a doctor after all. Surely, he could identify a hopeless case when he saw one.

Okay, I admit it. I did it out of pure vanity. I did it for my ego. I had this egocentric gut feeling that I couldn't just let this person go without a fight. My ego certainly was not going to allow me to so easily lose my first patient.

En route to the hospital, I formulated my plan: get several large bore IVs going, place a subclavian line, get blood, notify neurosurgery, notify orthopedics, get an assistant and IV antibiotics, get to the OR, and control the bleeding ...

Since I was unfamiliar with this hospital, I made my first mistake before I even reached the patient: I entered the emergency room through the waiting room area. As the automatic doors opened, there stood the patient's family, mother, father, and brother.

"Doctor!" they yelled in unison.

The mother approached me first. "This is our daughter!" Tears streamed down her face. "Please, please do not let her die!"

"I promise we'll do everything we can," I said, trying to slide around the mob the family had formed. "I promise I'll—"

"You don't understand," the father interrupted. "This is our only daughter. Don't let her die!" The last part didn't sound like a request. It was a demand.

As I left the waiting room, the ER doc was waiting. He looked ragged. "You know, Tom," he said, lecturing me already, "this is not a teaching hospital. We don't go through this kind of exercise on a corpse. No heroics, please."

I could hear the ER doc, but the words didn't register in my consciousness. Already in my mind, I was working on the mangled young lady I caught out of the corner of my eye at the end of the hall. As I quickly approached her gurney, the normal speed of life eased into slow motion. With her head and upper body so covered in blood, the poor girl was virtually unrecognizable as a person. I knew in that moment that if I proceeded as I'd planned, I would be getting in over my head and there was going to be no one to bail me out. On the other hand, wasn't this what I had spent the last thirteen years of my life preparing for? Wasn't this what I had intended when I first decided to become a surgeon in the first place? Yes, to both questions. But really, everyone in the hospital thought this girl was dead. What the hell was I thinking?

The truth is that I wasn't thinking. I was reacting as I was trained to react.

After obtaining an encouraging stabilization of her blood pressure and noting that her pupils still responded, I enlisted several nurses to help transport her to the operating room. Together we assembled the cardiac monitors, IV lines, and other paraphernalia required in such complicated cases. Off we went, running down the long corridor, past the nursing supervisor, and into the operating room. I knew that in a matter of moments we had to have this girl's belly open to stop the bleeding or she wouldn't survive.

By the time the anesthesiology team arrived, we had the patient on the table, prepped, draped, and ready for the incision. The nursing supervisor and ancillary personnel were in complete shock that something like this was happening in their hospital.

"Dr. Ashton," a nurse said pompously. "This is a for-profit hospital. We have to account for every item you're using here."

For the first time since I'd seen my patient, I pulled my attention away from her. I looked aghast at the nurse as I tried to assess whether she was serious.

I could see that she was. She wasn't simply looking down at me; she was scolding me for opening her precious stash of blue-packaged treasures (operating equipment). Once I saw that look, I determined that I would ignore her completely from that point on.

Right as I started the incision, I ordered more blood for transfusion. This would require a team of technicians setting up elaborate equipment behind and to the right of where I stood. When I looked up to see if I'd gotten a response, I saw exactly zero technicians getting to work.

Then finally a team of technicians entered the room. "Dr. Roberts said you may want to auto transfuse." Autotransfusion is done in cases that will require massive amounts of blood, like in ruptured aortic aneurisms. The procedure takes the blood that would otherwise be lost, cleans it, and gives it back to the patient.

"Yes," I said gratefully as I continued the incision. "Absolutely, yes." If this team hadn't miraculously appeared, the young lady would have died before I had a chance to begin.

The cut I made ran from stem to stern, resulting in a massive amount of blood to appear in the abdominal cavity. Without the auto-transfusion, we would never have had enough blood to keep her going. Thank you, Dr. Roberts, I thought.

I packed the entire abdominal cavity with large lap packs, placing pressure into all four quadrants. This gave us a brief respite from the crisis and allowed the anesthesiologist to stabilize her blood pressure. We now had a living, stable patient. The catheter placed in her bladder showed bright red blood instead of clear yellow urine, so I knew she had a bladder injury.

From here, I waited for a time so we could get caught up with her fluid requirements and let her brain perfuse. As long as we maintained the stable condition, there was still hope. After perhaps ten minutes of waiting, looking at each other, and enduring the incessant bitching of the nursing supervisor, I began my tour around the patient's abdominal cavity to assess the damages. Almost everything that could be broken was broken. I had experience with a few of these injuries, but never all at the same time. I had assisted in some of these operations, but I had never been here in this place, alone, elbow deep in blood, without five or six other surgeons, all specialists in their area.

Now here is why I believe I managed to overcome these deficits: I didn't think about what to do; I just did it. I didn't have the time or the luxury to think, plan, or understand. I knew only that I was dealing with an obvious bladder injury, a shattered spleen, a fractured liver, and on and on.

Repairing the liver is like trying to sew together two pieces of Jell-O. You need large blunt needles that can pass through the tissue without causing further damage. You need to proceed slowly and easily. And you need luck. A special argon laser to control capillary bleeding from raw liver surfaces is nice too.

"Do we have an argon laser?" I asked, not anticipating a positive reply.

"Yes, sir. It's ready."

I paused for the briefest moment, beside myself with confusion. Only minutes ago, I was hearing nothing but negativity. But in this response, I noticed a different attitude in the operating room. People were beginning to buy into the concept that maybe, just maybe, we weren't operating on a corpse after all.

I continued my investigation, finding much of the upper abdomen looking intact, including possibly the stomach. I noticed potential damage to the right kidney but decided to leave that be and hope the bleeding stopped on its own. With bleeding coming from so many other places, I had more important things to address.

A quick check found that the patient remained stable, so I decided to "run the gut." That's what we call the act of checking the intestines—all twenty-some feet of them to see if anything is leaking shit. Yes, I mean shit literally. When you run the gut and find shit mixed with blood, it's not a pretty sight. When I ran this girl's gut, midway down the small intestine I found a near-total disruption that spewed thick, brown-red sludge into the abdominal cavity. With the help of the scrub nurse, I repaired this first, and rapidly.

Next came the urinary bladder. I had never repaired such a rupture unassisted, so I found myself mentally crossing my fingers to make sure it would hold up. From here, it was organ after organ, my hands a blur of thread and sweat and blood. I was conscious of the voices in the room, but only responded subconsciously. All that mattered was repairing the damage.

Two eight-hour procedures and forty-eight hours of rest later, the young lady was stable enough to transport by air to the only neurosurgeon in the state who would accept her. Even when she left my hospital, I wasn't sure whether she would make it. The neurosurgery would require its own set of heroics.

As I write this, I'm happy to report that the young lady survived. The last I heard, she has graduated from high school, gotten married, and has two children.

This was a miracle.

I didn't realize it then, but I know it now. What I did that day was a miraculous thing. I wish I could take credit for it, but in reality, I was simply channeling the energies of Infinite Wisdom through the Universal Subconscious Mind. And I did so because of my ego. I was tapped in to the universal nature of all life and all knowledge and merely set an intention and focused on nothing else until the patient was flown away. I set this intention because my ego would not allow me to accept defeat. This is the all-powerful, good side of the ego, not egomania. This is the positive, service-oriented side of the ego. Even as I worked, I thought of nothing other than an image of this person well, alive, whole, and home with her family. In the end, that's exactly what we achieved.

This was the most exhilarating experience in my life. On the surface, I took the credit, but in my heart, I knew that I, working alone, based on my acquired skills, could not have accomplished so much. I had unknowingly used the powers of mental perception. My visualization preceded a manifestation, and my imagination made it so. The driving force was intention, and intention coupled with imagination is the secret to deliberate creation. I recognize now that the intention about which I write started decades before this event in my vivid imagination.

After years of experience and contemplation, I have finally concluded that this power of imagination is omnipotent, responsive in all situations, and responsive to literally everyone.

On that day, I learned three things. First, my ego plays only a small role in the act of doing. Yet my ego was essential to the initiation of the events that resulted in a miraculous outcome. Second, I learned not to be self-reliant, that true peace and true wisdom takes something more. And third, I learned that my intention is more powerful than my abilities. What I conceive (and what you conceive) can and will be done. We will discuss more on this subject in Chapter 4, but for now, keep in mind that mind precedes matter every time.

Even to the day after I helped that young lady survive, I knew I was on to something. But it took the next thirty years of surgical practice to understand what it was. Today, I'm going to tell you what it was. I'm going to tell you what it is. I'm going to make you aware of something truly special.

We can summarize that something special with just one sentence borrowed from the introduction of Power vs. Force by David R. Hawkins, MD, PhD: "The individual human mind is like a computer terminal connected to a giant database." In other words, your ego makes you think you're you, but in reality, you're simply part of a greater (and truly gigantic) whole. You are connected to everything and everyone, including Infinite Wisdom that created us all.

To achieve a full understanding of what this means, we must embark upon a study of awareness. This study, and the understanding that comes with it, will change everything for you, but only if you are ready/receptive.

Let's ponder that notion from Dr. Hawkins one more time: "The individual human mind is like a computer terminal connected to a giant database." Our challenge in the chapters to come is to access that database. You may think this is simply a clever analogy to get you thinking about things bigger than yourself. It's not. This is in fact the true nature of the universe. There is no more accurate

description of reality than this notion that we are all p:
of a greater whole.

You know what the best part is? You have autom
this giant database. You are in fact one with it already. The only reason you haven't fully tapped into it yet is that your ego-driven mind
has closed you off to this reality and may not allow you to perceive
or appreciate it.

So before we move on, let's try a quick exercise to keep your ego
in balance. Whenever you find yourself doubting the things you are
about to read and learn, return to this logical mantra to remind yourself that all thinking makes it so.

Think about the relationships between these words:

Essence

Awareness is the essence of intention Intention is the essence of
personal creation Personal creation is the essence of ending suffering Ending suffering is the essence of ending fear Ending fear is the
essence of love Love is the essence of a purposeful life Purpose in life
is the essence of light Light is the essence of the universe The universe
is the essence of you You are the essence of the universe.

This line of thinking represents the very power to create a new
reality. Using only your open mind and imagination, you can (and
will) take a quantum leap from where you are today. You will discover
for yourself the positive energy of your source, Infinite Wisdom, that
created the universe and connects us all.

If we can learn to accept the sequence of phrases above, we can
travel from awareness to a new reality. If you are serious about discovering your potential, read it again and again until it makes a connection with your imagination. By your deliberate thought processes, you
will conclude that your intention and imagination create your reality.
You are not a victim of fate or of any external influence. You are the
creator. Your power lies within.

And if you are serious about changing your life, read on to discover how to achieve higher levels of awareness.

CHAPTER 4

MIND POWER

When we think about life on earth, we can compare it to a trip to Disney World. That's right; life is like a brief but exciting stay in the Magic Kingdom. Just like when we go to Disney World, life has its fair share of challenges and setbacks. Sometimes the kids are fussy in the car ride over. Sometimes we have a hard time finding a parking spot. Sometimes it's difficult to get all our things together. Sometimes we're ready to crawl out of our skin by the time we get to the head of the long ticketing line. Sometimes it's too hot and we sweat through our clothes. Sometimes it's too sunny and we get sunburned. Sometimes it's too cold and we shiver all day. Sometimes the rides we want to experience are broken. Sometimes Mickey scares the pants off our children. Sometimes our ice cream melts all over our hands. You get the idea.

But just like that trip to the Magic Kingdom, even though there are headaches and difficulties along the way, the overall experience can be exciting and fun. It's all in how we choose to perceive it. Our Disney World experience (as in life) can be hot, muggy, crowded, expensive, irritating, and shallow; or it can be as it is in the minds of our children: enchanting, loving, exciting, and, yes, even magical. The difference exists within us, and we can control that area of our world through our mental perceptions. We can create our heaven or our hell.

Through our examination of awareness, we are going to discover how to do this.

Even in the Magic Kingdom, things can challenge our mood. Sometimes we see parents screaming at their children, everyone (mostly the adults) getting tired and grumpy, and, yes, it rains. But the children with their innocent point of view can remain above the chaos. They have a great time, no matter what happens. We, too, can regain that innocence (which is, by the way, our true nature). We don't have to learn how to do it; we just have to remember how to do it. There was, after all, a time in our lives when we were bright-eyed kids who lived above the chaos. Jesus said that unless we become as little children we cannot perceive heaven.

But what do I mean when I say "the chaos"? The chaos is all of the day to-day events we encounter or create in our lives. It's the chaos we read about, watch on TV, see at the movies, and experience at our jobs, in our relationships, and, more importantly, in our minds. The chaos is the never ending, negative self-talk, gossip, and conflict we surround ourselves with. If we can learn to pursue awareness of natural law and our connectedness to Infinite Wisdom, we can literally rise above the chaos. We can become like little children, always at peace, always full of wonder, always happy.

> And what a wonderful state of Being . . . to know with absolute certainty, the reason for your existence, and to have full realization of all that you are. And then, you get on with what you came to do: live your eternally expanding life in joy. (The Astonishing Power of Emotions, Ester and Jerry Hicks)

You may not agree that children are always happy. So, let me explain. A crying child or a grumpy child does not signal unhappiness. It is a learned behavior that results from temporary pain or discomfort. Notice that once the momentary problem is solved, the child immediately returns to a world of joy and wonder. That child intuitively knows how to live and react to the "now." They harbor no ill feelings or grudges and are skilled at living above the chaos. Given an optimal environment, a child's ultimate destiny is peace and joy. Given a "normal" environment, a child's ultimate destiny is an addiction to chaos just like ours.

So, let's get started, shall we? What's the first step? Well, the first step is to forget about everything that's contributed to the chaos in the past. Let's not be hindered by our past or even discouraged by our present. Instead, let's allow our future to pull us back into our true nature, which is what this book is all about, and removing the obstacles to this awareness is our mission.

One way to start this process is to examine our perceptions. After all, if we want to feel happiness, be at peace, and experience joy, these things have less to do with the facts than they do with our perceptions. Since our perceptions are determined by our automatic thoughts, core beliefs, and attitudes, if we want to be happy and joyful all the time, thinking literally makes it so.

Yes, you have heard this concept a thousand times. There's even a song about it. It goes, "Don't worry ... be happy." But there's more to it than that, of course. Making our lives joyful in this fashion can only be achieved through a process of awareness—awareness of how we are all connected, awareness of the true nature of ourselves and the world around us, and awareness that these truths become self-evident and useful, if only we embrace them.

Now, I can understand if you're feeling a little resistance at this point. In our human experience, it's common to be conscious yet unaware. Awareness is a choice we make as our experience expands and grabs our attention. This awareness is what makes our world a happy one or not. And as you will discover in the pages to come, where we are at this very moment in time—right at this very moment and right at this very time— is the perfect place to launch ourselves into the next level of awareness.

So, let us return to ourselves, to our original, default states of being, by choice. Let us choose to become aware and feel within our hearts that all is well. Doesn't that sound nice? It is nice.

Yes, I know it's hard to believe at first, but our happiness really does depend on our state of mind and not external events or circumstances. To realize this is to achieve what I call a grand awareness—grand because those external events and circumstances that represent the chaos are everchanging and usually outside our control. Everything changes. Our very presence in this life form is only temporary. We are born, we grow old, and then we die, passing back into the earth. In other words, this physical manifestation—all of what we know, hold dear, and value—is trivial compared to the eternity of the infinite state. In later chapters, we will learn that we belong to the infinite state. But first, we must learn about awareness before we can live in awareness.

We're Not from Around Here

"What?" you might say. "Are you saying we're all some kind of space aliens?"

We originate from space, yes. Aliens, no. What I am saying is that there is no such thing as space aliens or even this world. That we are living here on planet Earth, subject to our daily rigors, frustrations, and fears, is mere illusion. It is temporary, malleable, controllable, and only exists because we believe it is real. And we have created this reality for ourselves. What we perceive as life on Earth is merely the collective dreams of our souls (a collective form of energy, consciousness). When we die, it is less like a loss of soul and more like an awakening of soul. The soul (Universal Consciousness) awakens from worldly slumber and remembers with fondness its experience on terra firma, for it has been an adventure in evolution. One more entity has contributed its unique experience to the entirety of Universal Consciousness. In this way, Infinite Wisdom has known itself in a physical form.

Don't get me wrong; I am not suggesting that there is no such thing as the physical. Thinking makes it so, after all. We are indeed physical beings parceled from Infinite Wisdom, and we are experiencing this physical manifestation with no memory of our own innate perfection. We have chosen to be seemingly separate from God for a brief sojourn into a physical world, unaware of our relationship with the whole of existence.

So, as we move ahead in our journey toward ultimate awareness, remember two things. First, remember that consistent thought can and will become manifest. Remember also that our physical presence here— along with everything we focus on in our daily lives—is mere illusion, a product of our collective consciousness, our collective understanding of what the world is and what it should be. We are simply parked here in the physical realm for a brief opportunity to experience some things both good and bad. In other words, this world of physical manifestation is little more than entertainment and amusement. It's just a place to pass the time away, to experience and learn, to live and to die, and, unfortunately for most, to suffer (yet even suffering is a valuable experience). Any other perception of this life is distorted and perverted. We may think that our true nature is small and insignificant while the world of form is permanent, all-powerful, and real. Just the opposite is true.

Beyond All Reason

As a physician and surgeon, I was always cursed (or maybe it was blessed) with a need to prove everything empirically and based on science. Like many educated people, I preferred the security of my rationality and reason to the fearful acknowledgment of forces not obvious. But as Gandhi once said, "Experience has humbled me enough to let me realize the specific limitations of reason. Just as matter misplaced becomes dirt, reason misused becomes lunacy" (Gandhi's Way to God).

Not until recently did I decide to accept (in addition to my precious reason and science) those things that work, whether I understand them or not, and with or without a scientific basis. I decided to proceed with an appreciation of faith, as explained again in the writings of Gandhi:

> Start with the faith which is also a token of humility and an admission that we know nothing, that we are less than the

atoms, I say, because the atom obeys the law of its being, whereas, we, in the insolence of our ignorance, deny the law of nature.

This decision to accept something greater than reason (or even beyond all reason) did not come easily. It was forced upon me by my life experience and the realization that what I was doing simply was not working.

I try to avoid pontifications and any ego-based judgments upon any person, place, or event. All these things have served me well in my journey into awareness, after all, and we should all invoke a spirit of gratitude. But in my case, I have learned to accept a great many things I used to think I could change or control. I used to think that since I loved my wife, I could control her and the things I did not like about her I could change. I used to think that everything would go exactly as I planned. Life has taught me that I can't think this way and be at peace, so I am choosing peace. I accept and surrender and I feel better.

So, what is the first thing I learned about life beyond the shackles of reason, of life that takes certain things on faith? It is, above all, a life full of joy.

What constitutes a life full of joy? Does it require health, prosperity, and unconditional love? Or is this utopian fantasy also filled with disease, poverty, and hate? Are these conditions mutually exclusive or complementary? Which condition leads to joy and fulfillment/happiness? Is it possible that all these conditions eventually lead to the same place? Is it possible that no matter what happens or how you handle it, you can't possibly get it wrong?

Some of us seem to have attracted a disproportionate amount of chaos into our lives. Living in chaos and attempting to control the consequences has brought me to a remarkable realization: all of it served as the perfect motivation for me to move to the next step in the evolution of my consciousness. I have come to understand that everything that has ever happened to me (and I hope you will see to you) is a gift, a blessing. This is true no matter how I felt about the occurrence at the time.

The point is that before you can ascend to a higher level of awareness, you must set an intention—and assuming that the intention is in keeping with the overall direction of the universe, it must be positive, affirmative, loving, and not harmful to any sentient being. If you do this, well then that intention will be realized. Your thinking will make it so. You may not perceive this realization for a long while. You might not even agree with the initial outcome. But know this for a certainty: one way or another, your intentions will become your reality.

In Power vs. Force, Dr. Hawkins states, "Awareness is the allen-compassing attractor field of unlimited power identical with life itself. And there is nothing the mind believes that isn't erroneous at a higher level of awareness."

Hold on. What? Let's take a closer look at that statement. What Dr. Hawkins is essentially saying is that awareness carries potential for unlimited power. What would the awareness of unlimited power look and feel like in your life? Unlimited power sounds pretty good, doesn't it? I know it did (and does) to me.

If we hope to achieve that kind of power, we must first ask ourselves some questions. Is it possible to attain such a level of power? Is this state of awareness contingent on somebody of secret knowledge that only a few gifted individuals experience? And, moreover, what are the beliefs we currently have that become erroneous once awareness is achieved?

These are the questions that this book seeks to answer. I'm excited to help you find them.

The Illusion of Separateness

So, where are we headed? Well, eventually, we will come to know how awareness creates our sense of being (a being so familiar and yet completely intangible). Moreover, when we reach full self-awareness, we realize that our physical self is purely an illusion. This becomes obvious when we understand that nothing that changes can be real, thus anything that changes is illusion. The idea of illusion is difficult because, as we learned in the last chapter, your ego stands between you and truth. The ego says, "This is pure fantasy. You know you are real, and you know everything is cool just the way it has always been." But honestly, where has the ego gotten you? Maybe it's time to evolve your thinking.

Let's define the term illusion, shall we? An illusion is anything that is not real that appears to be real. It is interesting that our lives are based almost exclusively on illusions. At birth, we experienced a feeling of separation from the infinity of our Source. Yet since we are all one infinite thing, how could separation truly exist? The fear created by separation is based on an illusion; therefore, fear is an illusion. Does this not mean that we have nothing to fear? What are you afraid of? Any fear you can experience is not real. It's an illusion.

That's the trouble with our default brand of ego-based thinking. When we base our behavior solely on the illusions of time, space, and matter—when we predicate our thoughts exclusively (or even significantly) on the physical world around us—all we're doing is perpetuating the insanity that dominates our existence.

The "oneness of existence" is a concept that, once internalized as a lasting truth, can potentially transform life on planet Earth. How is it that there's no such thing as separate individuals? How is it that we are all one? Good questions. As an exercise of faith, let's follow these underlying principles:

1. The accepted science of physics describes the start of our time and universe as a big-bang event that occurred fifteen billion years ago.

2. Prior to that event, we really have no clue as to what was going on. But surely there was an entity to establish the circumstance for this granddaddy of all fireworks. If you prefer, let's call that entity an "energy." Some call it "consciousness." I call it "Infinite Wisdom." No matter what you call it, it's clear that this energy is present throughout infinity. It's also clear that this energy

is conscious because the big bang proved that it decided to do something. It created an event.

3. This infinite energy of consciousness is omnipotent.

4. To create the big bang, the consciousness that I call Infinite Wisdom essentially had an intention. The cosmos is the result of that intention. We all came from that same dream, so we are all one thing, evolving into different manifestations of that dream.

All the great thinkers of our time and for thousands of years have taught this oneness concept. Even Jesus said that we are all one. The way he described it is like this: the kingdom of heaven is within us and we are all brothers. No matter what name you give it, Infinite Wisdom is the Source of all that is. This one does not divide itself. This one has created matter. Life, as part of this matter, is created to perceive and experience Infinite Wisdom's magnificent creation. That same Infinite Wisdom has left it up to man to conceive his own reality, limited only by awareness. Intention fosters personal creation, and that leads to the end of suffering. It is the awareness of Infinite Wisdom that allows us to perceive and practice unconditional love (the end of suffering).

The God Particle

Throughout history, science in its strict method of investigation and proof has actually been wrong about the real-world 80 percent of the time (so far). One only needs to recall the theory that the earth is flat. If that's not ridiculous enough for you, consider the idea that people in the civilized world used to believe that witches exist. Based on the science of our state of understanding, I present the following:

All material things start with a thought (or vibrational energy similar to light). That vibrational energy is eternal while the resulting physical entity is transitory. The vibrational energy that permeates everything is available by a direct connection to us. It has been described as a matrix of energy that is ubiquitous throughout infinity.

We human beings are part of the transitory particle entities that were created by the vibrational energy. This same energy is present in our minds and connected to all other entities through Infinite Wisdom, the source of all vibrational energy that permeates the universe. Intuitively and emotionally, we can now formulate a working concept of the oneness of all things and how that relates to the world we have built within our mind.

If we know that all material things start with vibrational energy, and that vibrational energy is eternal, and if we know that the vibrational energy is the source for all physical entities, we also know a few interesting things. First, this "first" particle that resulted in the "first" vibrational energy still exists. Sometimes it exists as the tiniest particle you can imagine and sometimes the particle returns to pure energy. This we know from scientists who study particles as they appear and seemingly disappear.

In any case, the world as we know it today required just one event to begin its formation: one particle became two. The particles combined based on the physical laws of quantum physics. Then the particles became so many that the natural law that we call gravity brought the particles close together until the energy of attraction was countered by the energy of creation (nuclear fusion).

The big bang (or "nuclear fission-fusion," so much energy manifesting into solid stuff) was the nuclear-chemical reaction that set our physical universe in motion—and it all started with that single particle. That is why you and I and everything and everyone else represent the most magnificent physical manifestation that there could be in our physical universe. Better yet, we are part of the whole and part of each other and one with the universe because we all (everything) came from the same source. Later, we will learn that it is fear that prevents us from enjoying the benefits of these truths.

We all contain the same vibrational energy force that permeates the entire universe as we continue to evolve. This force constitutes the real us. Once we have a working knowledge of this, we can begin to understand that, based on our Source and the events here described, all matter is equal. Nothing is superior, and nothing is inferior. A human person is no more significant than an amoeba. And certainly, no man is superior to another. The illusion of superiority is a false concept.

Deepak Chopra, in Power, Freedom, and Grace, states,

> These particles give us the experience of matter through our senses, but they are not material entities. These particles are fluctuations of information and energy existing in a huge void. The particles constantly emerge from the void, come into creation, rebound, collide, and then disappear back into the void.

In other words, all things emanate from (and return to) this single Source. The fact that we have evolved into life forms with selfawareness and creativity makes us very special (but not superior) in the cosmos. We have become God's manifestation in this physical realm just as all things have, and we have become the latest version of God's greatest vision.

Now, the real us that we know from science consists of physical matter and vibrational energy. These two things are actually one and the same. Because vibrational energy makes up our thought processes and we can think with self-awareness, we have free will. We can come to an understanding of how to harness and use this free will for whatever purpose we want. We can screw up our lives or we can rock them out. Everything we encounter can either suck or rule. It's totally up to us. We call the shots. We have the power of the Source (Infinite Wisdom) because we are one with the Source. We the creation—we the people that contain the God particle—are all one and all perfect.

This world of vibrational energy communicating in our minds as thought and feeling gives us power to create anything. All the things you see around you at this very instant were created in someone's mind and made manifest. Even the plants, animals, rocks, and minerals were manifested from the mind (of Infinite Wisdom). Once you understand the power that you have based on this Source, you can be aware that this power is in fact the cause of every effect.

We are powerful because of our Source. What does that mean for you? For me, it means that I can relax. I can rejoice because I know that I am the latest version of God's greatest vision. I can know that any negative thought; perceived mistake, sin, or transgression; pain or misfortune; and any physical ailment were perfectly suited to get me to this super awareness. I can study and follow my true nature. Once my true nature is revealed and accepted, I can surrender to it, live above the chaos, and feel better.

Together we can replace our beliefs and self-doubt with selfacceptance. We can return to the state of grace we embraced during the first nine months of our lives before we were born. We can follow the same natural laws that created us and have sustained us from our first day on the planet until this very instant.

The Burden and the Joy of Self-Awareness

Unlike any other animal on the planet, we human beings are self-aware. We have earned the privilege to use this knowledge for good or for not. But what is awareness? Awareness is a mental process that relieves us of the detractors (negative thought patterns) and allows us to achieve self-validation so we truly live above the chaos. As our level of awareness increases, our reliance on past cultural influences subsides until at last we encounter the only true emotion, love.

Because awareness is a mental process, we know that it is also vibrational energy. Because it is vibrational energy (just like the God particle), it connects and is influenced by Infinite Wisdom. In other words, because we are self-aware, we can know for certain that we are one with Infinite Wisdom. There is no other way it could be.

That burden of self-awareness, however, is that it remains up to us to determine how to use it. We can use our awareness for good or for ill. If our actions and intentions are guided by love (as would be in accordance with the rest of the universe), we will reap the benefits. If our actions and thoughts are governed by fear (in other words, if we do and think things without full awareness), we will pay a price. What price? Well, for starters, we won't feel peace and joy.

The choice is simple: we can live in awareness or we can remain unaware. With awareness comes peace and happiness. With unawareness comes chaos, fear, and hopelessness. We choose. We create our own world. We create our own heaven and we create our own hell. Awareness of our own true nature, loving ourselves, and replacing the detractors with affirmations results in living above the chaos and converts chaos and insanity into peace and joy.

But what happens when we are not aware? Unawareness is essentially being unconscious. And we may even be conscious yet unaware.

It is our conscious self that is unconscious of some things most of the time and everything when we are in dreamless sleep. In contrast, the unconscious seems to be conscious of all things all the time. It never sleeps. That is to say, it is our conscious self that is unconscious of our unconscious and the unconscious that is conscious. When we speak of unconscious perception, we are speaking of events that we perceive but that we are not aware of perceiving.

Let's talk about conscious perception and unconscious perception for a moment. Unconscious perception is a form of vision without seeing. Our addictions and obsessions are examples of this. Any perceived negative self-evaluation or thought is being unaware of our true nature; we are zombies, and we function without consciousness. But you can, as an act of will, remove the veil that covers your mental vision. Consider this sequence of logic:

1. Since we are one with Infinite Wisdom, our hardware is perfect.
2. Defective software was loaded into our perfect hardware (the detractors).
3. Awareness can assure that our own perfection is part of our consciousness.
4. Being unaware is being unconscious, and that means we are unable to perceive the truth (blind sight).

5. Blind sight is perception without awareness. It results in fear, addictions, obsessions, and misery (the illusions). The chapters that follow will raise your level of awareness. Relax, be happy, and keep reading.

Our unconscious being conscious all the time and our consciousness being unconscious most of the time is a survival mechanism left over from eons of evolution. It allows us even today to perform mundane tasks while being fully alert and reactive to harmful or dangerous situations. It's like primitive multitasking. The problem surfaces when our conscious unconsciousness continues to be controlled by our faulty software from the past. We are controlled by this negative conditioning from the past, which forms our negative core beliefs, habits, and self-image.

It is difficult and complex to understand why we live that way, but we do. There are many things that contribute to our soft-wired unwillingness to follow natural law. Religion and our fanatical approach to survival of the fittest are two of these things. Our belief in scarcity and other illusions is another. Our early experiences and early environments have conspired to imprint our consciousness with these illusions that seem impossible to distinguish from reality (detractors).

Through awareness, we can deprogram the faulty software and download the good stuff. Delete, reboot, reprogram, and get back online.

It all comes back to the God particle and the power of creation that resides in everything. Energy vibration, thought energy, matter as manifestation—thinking makes it so. It comes down to understanding that anything, event, thought, experience, or circumstance is an illusion. The only reality is what you decide in your mind to be truth for you. And naturally, what seems true to you will depend on your level of awareness. It seems prudent then to seek out ways to increase your level of awareness.

Creating Our Own Reality

If we can take the above as truth, further scientific evidence leads us even closer to the significant concept that, through our own consciousness (which is the same consciousness of Infinite Wisdom), we can create our own reality. Science demonstrates that simply looking at an electron, for example, changes its properties. This might not seem like a big thing (electrons are quite small, after all), but make no mistake—this is huge! Think about this concept for as long as it takes to understand how huge this is. Simply looking at an electron changes its properties. You as a human being can look at something—indeed, one of the fundamental building blocks of matter and life—and make it change.

What does this mean? No small thing. It means that observation by human consciousness is an act of creation. When you look at an electron and it changes, it is consciousness that is doing the creating. Are you conscious? I think you are. Well, my friend, if you are conscious, you can create! And you do create. All the time. You create by your intentions on how you believe the day will pass. If you wake up thinking it will be a great day, it usually is. And if you wake up believing the opposite? Well, you know how it goes. True to your wishes, that's the way the day will pass.

Make no mistake. You have the power. You may not have the belief right now, but you most certainly have the power. Once the belief comes, you need no longer be the victim. Just as importantly, you will no longer feel the need to judge the people around you. You can and will accept and "be in the world, but not of the world."

Let's try a simple exercise. Tonight, as you fall off to sleep, set a positive intention for tomorrow. Imagine as best you can that everything you will do, encounter, achieve, and relate to (every person and thing) will result in a positive outcome for all. The more specific you are with your intentions, the better. This is what I do: I intend to be a source of love for every sentient being I encounter today. I intend to help someone today. I intend to be happy, and I intend to be healthy and wealthy. Do this visualization for a few days and I guarantee that you will see more positive occurrences in your life than before this exercise.

However, I must warn you that if your idea of a positive outcome is at the expense of another, or damaging to a relationship or the environment, you may indeed experience your positive outcome and feel victory, but not peace and joy. You will find that the Universe will give you what you think about or intend, good, bad, or indifferent, but you won't experience joy unless your intention is to go with the flow of evolution (which is always positive). If not, you will experience more pain and fear. If not, you will have created more chaos in your world.

Our Intentions

During my formative years, as is the case with most people, my family served as my primary influence. More directly, it was my parents' devotion to us and to their religious faith that shaped my young mind. My mother was Native American and my father was Scottish. Both sides of the family were prone to addictive tendencies, especially alcoholism. When my parents decided to have a family, they declared that the alcoholism "stops here." And you know what? It did. Their whole lives they lived free of alcoholism and so, too, their three children. All of this resulting from their intention.

Our faith certainly helped. We all went to church every Sunday and usually on Wednesday. Being young, I hated it, of course, but I still took the teachings of the church pretty seriously. In fact, I placed Jesus Christ high on my list of mentors and teachers. I saw him as the Great Physician, so naturally I wanted to become a doctor.

But herein lay the problem ...

We lived in a small town in the Bible-belt Midwest. There, when you finished high school, you either went to work in the steel mills, the coalmines, or the railroad. Going to college was rare. And medical school, forget it! Every aptitude test I took graded me out as qualified for most things, but medical school was not one of those things. I did make it through college, but with a C+ average. (By the way, I justified this average record by using the excuse that I had to work forty hours a week to pay tuition). Never would I get into medical school with a C+ average, especially in this era when schools had thousands of applicants for each position. Out of college with a BS degree in microbiology, I was drafted into the army, which meant Vietnam. I ran to the navy recruiting station and was accepted into OCS, where I would become a naval officer.

After four years in the navy and obtaining a master's degree in biology, I still could not get into medical school.

Having a strong background in science and an MS degree facilitated my move into teaching. The year I taught high school chemistry and biology was stimulating and challenging. The kids were wonderful and full of positive expectations. But my heart was not in the right place. I felt myself sliding deeper and deeper into a depressed state. I struggled with migraines as my overall health deteriorated. At the time, I thought the world had conspired against me. But I was wrong. In fact, the Universe was conspiring for me.

Finally, as I sat in my family physician's office, I confessed my unhappiness and disappointment to a confidant named Dr. Gagnini. His advice on how I might continue on my path toward becoming a doctor was simple. "You know, in Mexico, they would welcome you with open arms."

So, with eyes wide with excitement, I borrowed lots of money and went off to medical school in Mexico. I packed the Chevy Vega with as much stuff as possible and off I went with my wife and our three-yearold son. Sure, we were young and foolish. But you know what? We had an intention. And as I wouldn't learn until much later, intention is everything.

Funny thing, during all my preparations, it never once occurred to me that a school in Mexico just might teach in Spanish! Lucky me, there was a Spanish proficiency test I had to pass. For my first two weeks, I dedicated myself to learning Spanish. Two weeks might seem like way too little time to become proficient in a language, but remember, all our constraints are mere illusion. As long as we have intent, we can achieve anything. Well, I had intent. And I passed the test and started medical school.

I studied hard for two years before the miracle. In class, I happened to overhear this comment by a fellow student: "A major medical school in the United States is taking transfer students this fall." In that moment—a moment that changed my life—I realized that there was a slim chance I could get into an American medical school.

With that glorious thought on my mind, I ran home and called the school. I didn't ask for an interview; I demanded an interview. The secretary told me that there were no more interviews available.

My response was totally out of character for me. "I am coming," I said. "And I will be interviewed."

I still laugh when I think about what that secretary's face must have looked like when I said that. In any case, I got my interview to transfer to one of the top ten medical schools in the country—and it all happened because I refused to accept no for an answer. Since the secretary never actually scheduled me for an interview, I sat in the admissions office for three hours before anyone would even acknowledge my presence. Then, finally, it happened.

The interview was with a pathologist who had previously been a naval officer. Once he heard my story, he presented me to the admissions committee, and I was admitted with advanced standing. Today, I'm proud to say that my MD is from one of the top ten medical schools in the country.

Before I got in, though, I felt I was not qualified. I had thought that being drafted was the worst thing that could have happened to me. But by grace alone, I got into the navy. By grace alone, I was stationed where I could earn a master's degree while on active duty. By grace alone, I was interviewed by a retired naval officer. By grace alone, I graduated from one of the top medical schools in the country.

I tell this story to make several points. I hope listing these points here will help you understand where you are going with the Awareness Project.

1. Although our lives often seem to be confused and disappointing, this is not the case.

   That "seeming" is illusion. As I have mentioned, everything that changes is an illusion. Embrace this concept, and you will start to feel better. These difficult times, if not appreciated as divinely directed, have potential to cause great suffering. In reality, it is suffering that supplies the motivation to change. In reality, suffering is a blessing.

   According to Colin Tipping, in his book Radical Forgiveness (2008), there is meaning to all suffering. He states that in fact "Everything is purposeful, divinely guided, all intended for the highest good." What actually is happening beneath the illusion we perceive as confusion and disappointment is in reality something of a spiritual nature. Moreover, all suffering is an opportunity to heal and grow. If we come to believe this, we are just one step closer to accepting that everything is perfect (including ourselves).

   Previous to this miracle of obtaining admission to medical school and thinking that I was a failure, I felt frustrated and suffered daily. At that time, my mind was full of negative detractors. I was not living up to my own standards.

   The failure syndrome goes something like this: no energy, interested in nothing, feelings of hopelessness, hiding from friends, no ambition, self-pity, staring into space while seeing nothing, and spending time in bed lying in the fetal position. This was my prevailing negative thought process. Talk about a bad attitude. I was lost to the negative detractors.

   But an incident occurred while I was on active duty in the navy that would change this attitude. Facing a life-and-death situation has that power.

   When the captain of the naval station left the base, an officer would be assigned as officer of the day. This meant that in the absence of the captain, the officer of the day was assigned to act on his behalf for any incident that may occur. The day I was assigned as officer of the day seemed like any other. All was calm on the base. Then I received a call from the front gate that a marine guard was having a breakdown and thought he was back in Vietnam. He was in fact shooting at anything that moved. It fell to me to defuse this deadly scene.

I was nearly overcome by fear. Truthfully, my training as a satellite communications officer did not prepare me for disarming an armed and dangerous marine, and yet here I was, the acting captain, and it all fell to me to take action. My survival and the survival of this marine and possibly others depended on me. As I thought about this marine, I remembered that my brother was a marine. Once, many years earlier, he had told me something that this day would save my life. He told me that, above all else, marines are taught to honor and obey an officer. I put on my white dress uniform, complete with sword, and tried to look as commanding as I could. I kissed my wife and son good-bye and then drove to the gate with lights and siren blazing. I pulled up to the gate, knowing that this could be my last day on Earth, and exited the vehicle. When I was face-to-face with this frightened marine, he placed his gun to my chest.

Other security personnel took station behind him, but we were all frozen in time, as any movement from them would assure my death. Remembering my brother's words, I called the marine to attention and requested his piece (gun) for inspection. To my amazement, he came to attention and presented the piece to me with strict military decorum.

Facing death is a life-changing experience. This was not the first time I experienced this, nor would it be the last, but there is an amazing lesson here. Could it be that my conversation with my brother years earlier was a coincidence, or was it something more? I choose to believe that it was much more. Can you apply this lesson to your own life experience? Can you appreciate that everything is as it should be?

a. There is an Infinite Wisdom that permeates everything, every thought, and every action.

b. Acceptance and surrender to this Infinite Wisdom is the end of suffering.

c. Fostering a belief in Infinite Wisdom is a choice we can make in deliberate creation.

d. You control your own destiny through awareness of universal truths.

As another exercise, imagine for a moment what it would be like if we actually held a deep inner conviction that everything is perfect. It would mean that any adversity we experience, any abuse we may suffer or commit, any physical ailment or deformity, any heartbreak or disappointment, any pain, and any adversity isn't suffering; rather, it is something given to us to help us evolve. And if we believe that, it would mean that we are always supported by Infinite Wisdom of the universe. And it would mean that even death is a meaningless illusion.

Since there is so much chaos and suffering in our lives (and in fact throughout the planet), our short experience here is meaningless when compared to the infinite existence that stretches before us. Maybe the lesson here is to enjoy this brief worldly existence and relax into faith and joy, no matter what our sensory perceptions indicate.

With all that in mind, the first natural law that we should recognize in this book is this: whatever you come to believe is true for you is true. And you can believe whatever you choose to believe. My own belief was that I would become a surgeon, and even though the odds seemed against me, it is exactly what happened. That "seeming" was an illusion.

Your life journey will be a reflection of this belief. You are free to choose what is true for you no matter your parents, culture, race, or past. I chose against all odds to become a physician (my truth), a surgeon, in fact.

Such a belief would allow us to accept that our pain isn't merely pain but rather a signal that we are out of alignment with natural law. In this way, perceived pain will become the perfect motivation and opportunity to heal something. Within this new belief system, could it be that pain and adversity contains (in its true meaning) a message from the universe?

2. Setting a noble intention is like activating the universal database that connects us all. In this way, progress is inevitable.

   Setting a noble intention is like an exercise of the heart—of intuition and imagination—not an exercise of the intellect. And yet the intellect participates in anything we do. "If you do not choose to be wholly joyous, your mind cannot have what it does not choose to be" (A Course in Miracles, Helen Schucman). Your heart knows what it wants, but unless you set the intention by using your mind, nothing changes. You must let your heart rule your head. I intended to enter medical school, but first I had to pass a Spanish test. I decided that this was my only opportunity, so I seized it.

3. The only thing preventing you from evolving is your own choice to take your eye off the ball right in the middle of the game.

   This is where the faith we discussed enters the picture. This faith is not based on any religious teaching or organization. It is based on your innate understanding that, no matter what you do, the sun will still come up in the morning and will shine on you as it shines on everyone, the good, the bad, and the indifferent. This is the kind of faith that conforms to natural law. This faith allows us to function above our intellect, outside of pure reason. It is essential to learning and accepting higher levels of awareness.

4. Failure is mere illusion.

   Striking out does not mean failure as long as you stay in the game. Failures are not setbacks. Every "failure" leads to growth and experience and allows us to evolve.

5. Nothing is ever over until you declare it over.

   And even that can be a valuable lesson in the matter of setting a good intention. If you should give up on your intention, the result will be a vacuum soon replaced by some other intention. In the process, you will have grown, you will have expanded your experience, and thus, you will have not failed. Rather, you will have evolved.

The Manifestation of Separateness

"Manifestation" can be defined as the ability to move from a world based on fear and lack to a world filled with love and abundance. We can manifest our desires using the power of our minds in a positive manner. This is the essence of "thinking makes it so."

But how do we manifest? How do we move from that fearful world to the loving one? First, we must realize that every good idea is a direct, perfect expression from Infinite Wisdom. If we do this, we can set the intention before backing off and letting Infinite Wisdom work out the details.

It is difficult to identify with any of this hocus-pocus stuff about manifestation unless we fully appreciate how the universe, including our world, functions. If we think we know how the universe works, we are probably wrong. If we can come closer to an understanding of the true nature of the universe, our lives would change completely.

Based on ancient teachings of all the religions and philosophies, and recently discussed by many scientists and researchers, the universe consists of a massive field of energy. No matter which religion, philosophy, or scientific discipline you favor, the working theory is that this energy field is the ultimate source of "all that is." "All that is" includes all of the known and unknown entities of the cosmos and you and me. Think about that for a second. Everything (everything!) is connected and fueled by a single energy field. Amazing.

We have already discussed this energy field by another name: Infinite Wisdom. But this energy field does not merely stem from Infinite Wisdom. In fact, this energy is us. The amazing yet verifiable truth is that, as part of the all-pervasive energy of the universe, we as physical forms possess all the potential of that energy. This is exactly why one may say that we are created in the image of God. We have always known this through faith, but now we have a scientific viewpoint to lean on as well.

At the same time, because we have lived for eons outside this knowledge, we have been unaware of our own power. From the dawn of man, we have lived as though we were separate from the power and separate from each other. That's why sages tell us we are living in a dream world and won't be happy until we wake up. Fortunately, we can wake up through the teachings of this book. We just have to have faith and put in the work to reach higher levels of awareness. If we can do that, one day soon we will awaken.

You know what's interesting about this manifestation of separateness we have collectively projected onto the world? It is in fact that belief in separateness that forms the basis of our fear and misery. Because we don't recognize that we're all connected to the same source, we have more reason to fear "the other." This illusion is so well established in our culture and DNA that it has resulted in many other illusions that control the way we live and interact.

Egomania is the insane preoccupation with self-interest at the expense of others. The extreme version of this is fanaticism. Imagine if you will a world controlled by fanaticism. It would be a world that experiences extreme devotion to a cause or system at the exclusion of all others. This intolerance results in hate, greed, conflict, rape, robbery, and constant war. You need not stress your imagination, as this is the very world we experience and it is all based on the illusion of separateness and scarcity.

As we discussed in the previous chapter, the ego is only one-half of the human equation. It has helped us to construct a belief system based on survival of the fittest, us versus them, and on it goes into our insane lives as we experience the chaos and fear. But what is the basis of our fear? An illusion.

The idea that we are not one with each other and with God is an illusion. That's a difficult concept to grasp for most of us in our conditioned egocentric orientation, but it is only one of the many illusions that are all based on fear.

So, if we know all of the above to be logically true, why do we choose to accept such a painful and chaotic existence? There are many reasons. We may have low self-esteem and therefore low expectations. We may not expect much because we feel we don't deserve much. In this way, we force ourselves to be content to settle for less than the ideal.

By our very birthright, we can create whatever we allow ourselves to create. This actually happens every moment of our lives, as we create the good, the bad, and the ugly details of life on planet Earth. As creators, we choose what to create, and we do that by controlling (or not controlling) what we think about consistently.

From the Dhammapada, translated by Thomas Byran (Teachings of the Buddha, Kornfield),

> we are taught that We are what we think. All that we are arises with our thoughts. With our thoughts we make the world. Speak or act with an impure mind and trouble will follow you as the wheel follows the ox that draws the cart. We are what we think. Speak or act with a pure mind and happiness will follow you as your shadow, unshakable. How can a troubled mind understand the way? Your worst enemy cannot harm you as much as your own thoughts, unguarded. But once mastered, no one can help you as much, not even your father or your mother.

What is it you are thinking about consistently? Answer that question and you will understand why you are where you are in your life situation.

As a little exercise, take a few minutes, put this book down, and make a list of the negative thoughts you have on a daily basis. Really, make a list. This list will be very revealing to you and may even offer some insight.

I'll provide a few examples about the kinds of things you may be thinking. We could make the following list as long as forever because we talk to ourselves in our thoughts 24/7, even while we sleep. But for now, let's just think about a few things that might be holding us back from our higher level of awareness.

"I'm fat."

"She doesn't like me." "I'm going to lose my job."

"My car will break down soon." "I can't stand him."

"I will never be able to do this." "This is all wrong."

"I'm so bad."

"I don't deserve it." "I'm lazy."

"I have no imagination." "I can't do math."

"I'm bad at business." "This is a bad idea."

"This will never work out." "I'm an idiot."

"Can you believe she said that?" "I'm addicted."

"I'm so old."

"I'm tired."

"That's depressing."

I guess you get the point but contemplate your own list. How would any sentient being react in such a consistently negative environment? Are these the kinds of negative-energy impulses you're sending to your subconscious mind? If so, how can you expect anything but negative energy to surface? You would be, in this case, creating your own set of negative detractors.

Here we see in action one of the natural laws. Countless authors have stated this law in countless different ways, but here is my own phrasing: you get what you consistently think about. This is how we create our lives, good or bad. Thinking makes it so.

The worst part is that our culture and the people around us make it incredibly difficult to embrace a new manner of thinking. It's so much easier to accept the thought patterns of our family, friends, and culture. If we blindly accept the existing norms of our culture, religion, or peer groups, we are allowing forces outside ourselves to create our reality.

Instead, I suggest we begin to embrace a process of deliberate creation. Deliberate creation is about personal choice. Personal choice is personal power. Personal power is positive when we recognize it as a gift from Infinite Wisdom.

How does deliberate creation work? It starts as all entities start: a conscious decision to delete negative detractors (thoughts). Then it evolves by using our imagination to visualize exactly what we intend to create.

This brings us to another important natural law: when you choose higher, positive, and affirmative thoughts, the conditions of your life must change.

Surrender to Advance

As a final message to this chapter—and a final concept to consider as we move into our examination of the various levels of awareness—remember that, as we move forward, we want only to attract good things into our lives. To do this, we must consistently think good thoughts and imagine favorable outcomes (deliberate creation). If we want to stay where we are (or even have things get worse for us), we should continue to think negative thoughts. But who wants that? Not me. What I want is positivity. What I want is to evolve.

Before we close, let's do another little exercise. List your negative thoughts in one column and create a positive thought. Take a quick look at some negative thoughts side by side with their positive counterparts. As you move forward with your study of awareness, whenever you hear yourself thinking one of these negative thoughts, do your best to shift your mind-set toward the positive. Only with a positive mind can we manifest positive things—and achieving a higher level of awareness is an incredibly positive thing.

Negative Thought	Positive Thought
I am sick.	I am healthy.
I am poor.	I am wealthy.
I am unhappy.	I am happy.
I hate people.	I love people.
I am a lone wolf.	I am a social butterfly.
Love means control.	I love unconditionally.
I am stuck.	I am free.
People take advantage of me.	I serve with pleasure.
I hate my job.	I love my job.
I hate change.	I am growing.
I work too hard.	I am thankful for all I have achieved.

The above might seem elementary and simple at first glance, but unless you can learn to control these thoughts, nothing will change for you. That's not what we want, of course. What we want is positive, constant change. My greatest desire is for you to lead a better and more peaceful life through a higher sense of awareness.

So, now you know what the hocus-pocus is all about: accepting natural law, understanding that you are one with Infinite Wisdom and with all things, and placing constant and consistent positive thought and intention back into the "database" that connects us all. As we move forward, real change will require you to put faith in Infinite Wisdom. It will require you to imagine and believe in positive change. It will require that you act as though your desires have been met already.

This might feel like surrender, but as you learned previously, surrender is a far better state of being than constantly worrying about the details of your chaotic life. We must surrender to Infinite Wisdom if we hope to find peace. We must surrender to advance as human beings.

Returning to our analogy of the flow of a river, remember that the ultimate flow of our lives is always toward our Source, and yet, as events unfold, there seems to be an ebb and flow. Sometimes we try to move against the flow and we waste our energy. Ultimately, we must submit and "go with the flow." Here is your exercise: stop wasting time and energy on deeds and attitudes that you instinctively know are against Infinite Wisdom. Practice the positive thoughts and banish the negative.

With that in mind, allow me to close the chapter with a piece of marvelous news: once you have developed an innate understanding that you and Infinite Wisdom are one and the same, how can there be any doubt that the ultimate outcome of this study will be anything short of a spectacular success? Infinite Wisdom is perfect, after all—and so, too, are you. Getting to that understanding is what this book is all about.

Oh, and one more thing. As we move forward with this study, remember to keep your intentions positive, but also remember to take action. Let's say you want to become a successful and well-known artist. Well, if that is your intention, the only thing you can do is get your ass in gear and start painting something. Existing in a world of positive thinking without action is like living in a la-la land of pure fantasy. Sure, thinking makes it so, but thinking without action will never be anything more than a dream.

And so, like Infinite Wisdom on the cusp of the big bang, let's get ourselves in the action business.

PART II

THE FOUR LEVELS OF AWARENESS

CHAPTER 5

THE FIRST LEVEL OF AWARENESS: SHAME/GUILT/FEAR/PRIDE

Before we delve into the nature of this first level of awareness, I would like to mention that the basis for our understanding of the levels of awareness as a process begins with the work of David Hawkins, MD, PhD. Dr. Hawkins has extensively studied the effects of universal attractor energy fields on human muscle response, kinesiology. He describes the method of testing and calibrating human muscle response like so: The individual subject stands erect with one arm extended to the side, keeping the arm parallel to the floor. A second individual conducts the muscle test by pushing down on the extended arm. A positive field created by a truth allows human muscle strength to test out as strong. The subject easily resists the downward pressure. A negative field (a false concept or negative idea) causes weakness and the subject cannot easily resist the downward pressure.

Using this system, anything or any concept can be calibrated based on its energy fields, usually from a scale of zero to one thousand. Advancing from one level to the next increases one's personal power. Not to worry; I am not going to ask you to advance through one thousand levels of awareness. As the title of Part II suggests, there are merely four. Rather, I have grouped what Hawkins calls his "seventeen attractor field levels" into four distinct groups. They are as follows:

First Level of Awareness: shame/guilt/fear/ pride

Second Level of Awareness: courage/acceptance/grace/reason

Third Level of Awareness: love/joy/ peace

Fourth Level of Awareness: Enlightenment

I am greatly looking forward to helping you advance through the four levels of awareness, but as with any endeavor, we must begin with some basic concepts. So, let us examine in this chapter some ideas about the first level before finishing up with a few contemplations and suggestions on how we might embrace these truths and move on to higher levels.

Most of humanity functions (or rather, malfunctions) on the first level (shame/guilt/fear/pride). This level is negative, destructive, and pervasive. Through its own marvelous and yet vexing self-awareness, humankind has evolved into the only sentient beings on the planet capable of this dubious distinction. If we use Hawkins's scale, this level tests out in the calibrations below two hundred (using the method of kinesiology as described).

What does a nearly complete lack of awareness (first level) look like? For an up-to-date report and detailed description, simply watch the news or read a newspaper. According to extensive research into the concepts of awareness, Dr. Hawkins calculates that nearly 80 percent of the world population functions at lower levels of awareness. This indicates that most of the planet wallows in a quagmire of shame, guilt, and fear.

This intriguing concept certainly seems to explain why our lives swirl in an environment of chaos. And it explains human history. Yes, it most certainly explains the events you will watch on the news tonight and almost every article you will read in tomorrow's newspapers. Given that the world functions mostly in fear, it is an absolute miracle that we have not already destroyed each other and our planet. I guess the jury is still out on this outcome. We do, after all, seem to be getting closer all the time. But if we hope to stave off that terrible eventuality, our goal must be to raise the prevailing level of awareness and save the planet. This dream is not a naive notion of wishful thinking. Rather, this awareness is the direction into which our species will evolve (eventually).

To begin our search on how to do that, let's examine the central source of all negative human motivation and get to the bottom of that central engine that drives the chaos in our lives.

Fear

The most important motivator in level one that we can discuss is fear. Fear may be the basis of all the other motivators and is therefore the most destructive. So, what is fear? And where does it originate?

In a nutshell, fear is the granddaddy of all illusions. The only reason it has such power over us is because of our enduring belief in it. As we learned in Part I, humankind believes in many illusions. The result is almost always fear.

To get to the bottom of fear, let's take a look at our early environmental and cultural influences. Pretty much all of this guarantees that we will live in fear. As an interesting exercise, think of your own fears and their origins. Then decide if these fears are based on fact or based on fantasy.

My fear: Its origin—fact or fantasy?

1.

2.

3.

4.

5.

Have any of these fears ever resulted in a negative outcome? Have they restricted your life experience? For example, my mother was afraid of water. She would never swim or even get on a boat. As a child, she was taught to never go near the river. A negative detractor was set in place that resulted in her phobia of water. Yes, this fear was essential in protecting her young life, but as she became trapped in her belief, she stored this negative detractor so obsessively into her subconscious that she could never enjoy any activity associated with water.

Fear is the granddaddy of all illusions, and belief in any of the illusions always leads to fear. Let's take a close look at fear. Neil Donald Walsch in his groundbreaking book Communion with God describes the ten major illusions: need, failure, disunity, insufficiency, requirement, judgment, condemnation, conditionality, superiority, and ignorance. Your exercise now is to list these illusions and examine how each one (if believed) allows fear to rule.

1. Need: Do you fear that you will never fulfill your needs?
2. Failure: Are you afraid you may fail?
3. Disunity: Do you feel that you are in constant conflict?
4. Insufficiency: Do you fear that there is never enough for you?
5. Requirement: Do you feel you cannot be or do something?
6. Judgment: Are you afraid that someone will find you lacking?
7. Condemnation: Do you fear what someone might think about you?
8. Conditionality: Are you afraid you may not meet the standard?
9. Superiority: Do you feel inferior?
10. Ignorance: Are you afraid that you don't know enough?

Note that each illusion is a two-way street. You may feel the fear or you may create the fear in another. Both scenarios have created suffering and chaos. The miracle is that, once we gain awareness of and understand the illusions, we can live in love and without fear. Think of your mind as a storehouse of the illusions (detractors). We can change our minds by withdrawing our interest and energy from that storehouse. This is the ultimate goal of your project, so keep in mind that this is your intention.

Beyond All Fear

You are now in the process of moving to a new level of awareness. Wow! All you had to do was to acknowledge the notion that you live in a world of illusion and that your ability to move past that illusion rests on your capable shoulders. Hopefully, you began doing just that during Part I, but here, just by recognizing the illusions that pervade your lives—and just by demonstrating a willingness to move beyond fear—you are ready to begin your advancement to higher levels of awareness.

I like to use an analogy to demonstrate how opening our perceptions to an enhanced awareness can facilitate power over our circumstances. Our lives can be compared to a journey that begins at birth. This represents the launching of our ship into the ocean of material form. We arrive with no knowledge of sailing our ship of life, so our parents and caregivers serve as captain of our ship. They essentially command all aspects of our journey.

As time passes, we begin to move up the ranks from deck hand to finally one day become the captain of our own ship. Sometimes we make poor decisions and sail into dangerous waters laden with hidden obstacles. Our ship flounders, but it does not sink. We survive to become seasoned and experienced captains, and we set out again. We hoist our sails, but alas, we have entered calm seas with no power to advance.

This is the forbidden zone from which few ships escape. We feel trapped by our habits, addictions, and negative detractors. We live in fear. We feel trapped by our unrealistic fears. Yet because of our innate courage and determination, we set our sails high in expectation that soon the miracle of favorable winds will once again fill our sails (we discover a book or perceive a significant experience). We banish fear by submitting to unknown forces, like Infinite Wisdom (faith and surrender). We banish fear by facing them head on as I was forced to do on the pyramid and by an awareness of our true nature and perfection.

Have you discovered your true nature? Have you elevated your awareness past the first level? We are motivated to continue the journey. This secret drive, this awareness, assures our survival and ultimate success.

The unknown force you are submitting to is Infinite Wisdom. Understanding your connection to the creative powers of the Universe is the key. You are one with Infinite Wisdom, you are perfect, so what is there to fear?

Make no mistake; once you move into that higher level of awareness, you will never be the same. You will change for the overwhelming positive. You will evolve into a new being based on this new knowledge.

But you must remain alert, ready, and receptive. The winds of destiny will move you forward only if you have the courage to hoist your own sails. The winds will come, but you must be receptive. Your intention stimulates your imagination, and you ultimately sail smoothly and effortlessly into your destiny thus created.

As one ascends in awareness, moving forward is a matter of choice. We have learned that we are, after all, creators of our own destinies. "Our choices set the context for our action, thus the possibility of a new context arises when we choose" (The Self-Aware Universe, Amit Goswami, PhD). We are not machines. We have and can exercise our free will. We can delete the faulty software that was mistakenly and innocently loaded into our hard drive—all that software that tells us to live in and be motivated by fear.

You know what else is great about this process? Once a new awareness is achieved, you can never go back. That is, as your awareness matures, you cannot become unaware.

The time and effort required to move up the ladder of awareness is an individual choice. Some individuals choose to remain unaware because they feel that a certain level is serving them and their perceived needs well enough. Some individuals would prefer to remain in their past thought patterns due to strong ego-based habits and negative beliefs. These belief systems are, of course, the product of domestication, culture, and peer pressure. Not only is this mentality a learned behavior, most probably, it is also part of our genetic code.

The first step is easy because that step requires only that you embrace the possibility of the illusions in which you live. But the next steps can be quite difficult for most people. Breaking such widespread and deeply ingrained thought processes takes work, dedication, and complete surrender to the process.

Take heart. I know you are ready for this work. The change in perception is open to you as it is for everyone. If you really want to step away from your fear, keep reading this book because that is exactly what we are going to do.

But if work, study, dedication, and surrender to a new process scare you—or seem like something you would rather avoid—join the crowd. You are still living in fear, as most of us are. Perhaps only one in ten thousand people exposed to this information will even attempt to apply it seriously. There's good reason for this: it takes courage. But then again, in case you didn't notice, courage is part of an advancing awareness. Having courage to attempt this is, well, exactly what you need to accept more energy from Infinite Wisdom and advance to the next level.

You will need this energy, for if you lack complete surrender to the process, chances are great that your relatives, friends, and colleagues will distract you from your goals. The fact that your early childhood environment, education, and even DNA have all conspired to keep you in fear only adds to the distraction.

How do we avoid these distractions? Dr. Hawkins teaches a simple approach to advancing the level of consciousness (and thus awareness). He suggests that since all truth is contained even in the simplest of truths, practice just one truth on a consistent basis and all truth will be revealed. Here is how I advise you to proceed, here is your new exercise: kindness is truth, so practice this one truth, kindness, for thirty days.

Practice kindness to all of creation. Surrender to the concept of kindness and through the grace of Infinite Wisdom, you will transcend your ego-based fear and all those other negative forces swirling around you. I suggest also that you approach this journey in complete humility. You need help, we all do. This is the human condition. As we embark upon the contemplations of this level of awareness, be humble and surrender.

Contemplations on the Level of Awareness

Answer the following questions so you may put in your own words your understanding of the concepts discussed above. The questions may seem silly or obvious at first, but your answers represent an important part of the process in your journey from unawareness. In these truths, you will find the key to transcend the chaos in your life.

1. Did you consciously choose the time and circumstances of your birth? _____

2. Did anyone anywhere make such a choice for himor herself?

3. Did you have any choice in your race, inherited characteristics, family, or cultural environment? _____

4. Is there anything you really need that has not been provided for your existence on this planet? _____

5. Does this thought process change in any way the feelings you may have had concerning other races, cultures, or religions? _____

6. Are you open to the concept of cleansing your mind of beliefs and attitudes that were forced upon you by your early environment? _____

Some Thoughts on Awareness

Instead of focusing on the negativity in your life, foster a spirit of gratitude for nature and the natural laws that have assured your continued sustenance and ability to read, think, study, learn, change, and serve. Research the concept of gratitude and think about the benefits of expressing it. Research the concept of grace as well. What might it mean to live in a state of gratitude and grace?

*A man's life brings nothing unless he lives
in accordance with the universe.*

—Tao Te Ching

CHAPTER 6

THE SECOND LEVEL OF AWARENESS: COURAGE/ACCEPTANCE/REASON

The second level of awareness includes the concepts of courage, acceptance, and reason. You know what's interesting about courage? Courage takes courage and also creates courage. Attempting to have courage to change gives you the courage needed to change. This is another gift given through grace from the Universe. It defines you as a human, descended from divine origins.

To get to the bottom of the second level of awareness, we should return to the concepts of Dr. Hawkins. Recall that the first level of awareness calibrated at two hundred. The second level begins above two hundred. At this level, we begin to experience power. Everyone becomes strong in response to the life-supportive fields above two hundred. We are keenly aware that fear is not going to rule our lives. We turn away from these negative influences and have the courage to move toward acceptance (surrender) and reason (for we are now using higher cognitive abilities).

We can define courage as bravery, will, intrepidity, and fortitude. It is the ability to confront fear, pain, risk/danger, uncertainty, or intimidation. Moral courage is the ability to act rightly in the face of opposition, shame, scandal, or discouragement. Yes, it will take courage and complete surrender to raise your level of awareness. Courage is one of those ideals that might seem impossible when you're still operating out of fear. Courage may be the complete opposite of fear, or maybe they can coexist, but one always predominates. Courage is commonplace in advancing awareness.

Consider this: Have you ever failed at anything before? Anything at all? It doesn't matter if we're talking about striking out in a Little League game or losing a big account at work. Have you ever failed at anything? Of course, you have. We all have. When you failed at that thing, did you run off and commit suicide? Of course, you didn't. And since that is true, it is also true that you have courage. The amount of courage depends entirely on your proximity to the second level of awareness, but you do have courage.

There's something else I'd like to point out about that failure you experienced. If you have ever failed, you have been gifted. The gift of tragedy is the gift of opportunity. This is a perfect demonstration of a natural law of the universe. Adversity and failure give us the perfect motivation to change, learn, transform our lives, and advance.

Grand Example of Failure Turning into Triumph

In 1776, Great Britain was the most powerful nation in the world. As a nation, it had spread its language and culture throughout the globe. There was, however, a rogue colony to the west that was challenging the authority and the sovereignty of the king. We know the result of this greatest of failures for Britain. It lost the war and what was to become the United States of America. From the British viewpoint, this was a great loss indeed—and on any scale could be judged as a negative event in their history.

But by 1945, Britain's greatest failure became its salvation. This same United States of America came onto the scene and helped rescue not only Britain but also the entire world from the tyranny of Hitler and the Axis powers.

So even on a grand and massive scale, failure does not mean defeat. Failure can indeed result (and in fact has ultimately resulted) in our greatest successes. This idea is more important to your awareness than you may realize. This one awareness has the potential to change your belief system. Think and reason yourself into this next concept. Remember your most devastating failure. Remember how you felt. Did you get angry? Did you cry? Did you seek vengeance against an adversary? Does this remembrance make you feel sad, worthless, or defeated?

If you answered yes to any of these questions, it means you must now reason yourself out of this box we call fear, but it takes courage to do so. Based on what we have learned, may I suggest a sequence of reasoning that can dissolve your negative feelings (detractors)?

1. You are the latest version of God's greatest vision.
2. You are a fully developed adult manifestation of perfection.
3. You are the son/daughter of the sun and the earth.
4. The omnipotent energy force places before you only what is perfect for your evolution and growth.
5. You cannot fail and you have never made a mistake.

   Note: Your exercise for the moment is to answer in the affirmative points one through five.

I know it seems on the surface as a ridiculous scenario. That is, unless you are aware.

The True Nature

The awakening moment for the second level of awareness as we roam the earth in a zombie-like existence may occur when we come to discover our true nature. It may be that you don't know your true nature, so let's start at the beginning of you and see if we can figure it out. But before we begin, you must agree to certain basic facts or assumptions:

1. You are now here, living on planet Earth, as a physical being.

2. Before that, you were nowhere.

3. Somehow you got from nowhere to here.

4. You are not aware of any conscious decision as to when and how you got here.

5. You are closely related to your father and mother, at least genetically.

6. It is good to be here.

7. Since you are still alive, you have chosen to be here (at least for now).

If you agree with these obvious assumptions, you can begin to experience the second level of awareness. You can agree that this is, after all, a good life. Everything we actually need has been provided. We just show up and nature takes care of us.

Don't believe me? Well, then, consider this example: What do you need in order to breathe? Oxygen, of course. Oxygen is a fundamental requirement for you to continue to exist in this physical realm. Now here's the interesting part: Where does that oxygen come from? From the plants that nature has provided. In other words, nature has provided you with something you need long before you even knew of the need.

Let's take that idea one step further. What do you need in order to carry the oxygen through your bloodstream? Iron. The iron in your blood that carries the oxygen came from the cosmos. In other words, out from the very reaches of the universe has come the perfect vehicle to sustain your life. And all of this came into existence billions of years before you ever had a need.

Still not convinced? Consider the very elements required for life on earth. All living things on this planet are carbon-based. Do you know where this carbon (the building blocks of all life) came from? Billions of years ago, deep within millions of stars, massive nuclear reactions created carbon. This same carbon is now the basis of, you guessed it, you. In other words, you are a "star being."

Remarkable, right? It's more than remarkable. The notion that you are created from the same stuff as stars and that everything you need in order to survive has been provided by the Universe is called grace. Through grace alone we have come to be.

Day Number One of our lives was quite amazing. Mom and Dad had recently had sex. This is hard to imagine (and maybe a little disturbing to picture), but it's true. That's what happened. Honest. Dad's deposit— which for him at the time was pure fun and delight—allows a sack of vibrating energy (millions of tiny swimming packets) to start a journey in a dark, wet, warm place. I'm not making the picture any easier to think about, I know, but bear with me. Mom's place, meanwhile, was perfectly prepared for our arrival. Although we had no idea where we were going, we knew we wanted to move north. At this time, moving was all we knew how to do. But you know what's interesting? Moving and wiggling is all we needed to know how to do. Nothing in the world would have served us at that time, save for moving and wiggling—so that (and only that) is exactly what we knew how to do. We wiggled our little tails so hard and fast that it propelled our DNA-filled bodies to the exact place we needed to be.

I suspect that you have no recollection of this most momentous event. Not one of the billions of human beings, living or dead, has any conscious knowledge or control over this event. In this physical arena, you did not choose to be created. And contrary to some spiritual disciplines that teach otherwise, you are not aware that your soul chose the time and place of your birth. There is no way we can know this for sure, and if we have no recollection of this, how does this knowledge serve us?

It was through grace that we came to be. We had no control over this process or recollection, but it was an essential event to our physical existence. And yet grace alone provided us with that perfect moment of existence, that opportunity to start our lives in this singular place and time. Grace, in other words, did something that should seem impossible and is at the least one of the most beautiful and inspiring things imaginable. So why is it then that, as intelligent, adult human beings, we don't continue to depend on the grace of nature? Why can we not put our faith in the Infinite to support the finite with this same original grace?

If you stop to think about it, you may just realize how full of grace your life really is. And if you stop to think about it, you might just find yourself advancing in awareness. Understanding and embracing the concept of grace is another moment that will take your awareness higher.

A Story of Grace

On Christmas Day 1963, I was driving from my hometown to visit my sister and the rest of the family for our traditional Christmas dinner. December in eastern Ohio can be cold and wet, and the roads can be covered with ice and extremely dangerous. This Christmas morning was just such a day. The rain on Christmas Eve had formed a thin, invisible layer of ice over the roadway.

As I approached a turn in the road, I lost control of the car. Nothing I did had any effect on my direction or speed. By the time I began drifting to the left side of the road, I was already traveling backward. From the direction I had been heading, I knew that the steep banks of the Ohio River were somewhere below. As my heart raced, my car caught sideways in its momentum and toppled down the bank toward the river. In those days, we didn't have seatbelts, so when the car began to roll, my face smashed into the ceiling, then into the windshield, then into the backseat, and then back up front into the steering wheel. Yet, as I was battered around, the only thing I recollect thinking about was relaxing, letting go, and asking God for help.

Later, I learned that the call a passerby made to the fire department suggested that someone would have to come to fish a dead body out of the river. The accident was so gruesome that someone believed there was no hope, that I was surely dead. But I wasn't dead. I had no out-of-body experience. I only experienced darkness.

When I awoke in the hospital emergency room, I learned that none of the doctors could find a single injury anywhere on my body.

Although I had endured an end-over-end roll into the Ohio River—and although I had experienced the chilling cold of those December waters—I was none the worse for wear. I spent the night in the hospital for observation, but I was fine.

On that day, I was the undeserving recipient of the grace of Infinite Wisdom. I didn't realize it then, but I believe it now. I was eighteen years old at the time, so naturally I just assumed that I was lucky. But in such times, I believe we are ushered along in our physical existence by the same grace that sustained us in the womb. And the second level of awareness assures that we have the wisdom to accept these gifts of grace. Now that I am a bit older and have had some experience outside that comfortable environment, it seems appropriate to ask who or what (even before conception) was that little thing moving and swimming and then ultimately joining and growing? And since that entity received grace, why would not that same grace reside within forever?

More importantly, if we want to awaken to who we truly are, shouldn't we start there? Yes, we should. And to get us there, we should examine the research in the fields of the biological sciences, physics, chemistry, quantum physics, and natural law (nonlinear physics). Examining these disciplines helps us arrive at scientific fact, not a nebulous body of fuzzy spirituality. If we can come to accept the findings of these disciplines, we can enhance our understanding of and relationship to each other and, indeed, Infinite Wisdom.

Those little swimming things filled with DNA that came from your father are made of complex combinations of carbon, hydrogen, and nitrogen (and other elements, of course) held together by chemical bonds. Chemical bonds are created by the movements of tiny, electrically charged particles called electrons (and other particles with quirky names). These particles orbit other tiny particles that make up the nucleus. The scientists who study quantum physics have determined that these particles are essentially energy packets in the form of vibrations. Unbelievably, the particles move from "there" to "not there," in and out of physical existence, constantly appearing and disappearing. As I mentioned earlier, scientists have also learned that the act of observing these events actually alters the activity of these vibrating energy entities. In scientific terms, this is described as the "unified field." Stated another way, it means that everything in existence is connected through this field to everything else. We are all one because we all come from this same unified field of constantly interacting subatomic waves and particles.

So, these elements that were delivered by Dad to Mom were simply little packets of vibrational energy. And waiting inside was another little packet of vibrational energy that Mom made available from her side. The combination of these vibrational energies became a new person: you. Then, for nine months, you lived in complete bliss—no worries, no striving, just being and growing and living in grace. Put another way, you were completely sustained by natural forces. This brings us back to our first law of nature: Creation, growth, and life have been handed to us on a silver platter. This idea is applicable to every living thing, every person, everywhere.

You know what is truly remarkable about all of this? This energy was assembled for us without even the slightest hint of concern or care on our part. We came from a massive supply of vibrational energy. We were organized into a physical being, sustained perfectly, and given life as a gift of grace.

"When you were born, your mind was completely innocent. You had no concepts about good or bad, right or wrong, beauty or ugliness; you had no concepts at all" (Don Miguel Ruiz). As we discussed in the introduction, our clean slate was then contaminated by our culture, society, experiences, and religion. At this second level of awareness, our goal is to wipe this slate clean and recall that innocent, carefree existence.

A child is born with the innocence of a pure consciousness and then is programmed with society's input. The child innocently believes anything he or she is told. "The unprotected consciousness of the child then becomes prey to the collective ignorance, misinformation, and fallacious belief systems which have blighted man's capacity for happiness" (Dawkins, 2008). I am not suggesting that you abandon your culture, religion, or family traditions. I am recommending that you add a new perspective to these concepts and enhance your experiences within these newly remembered parameters. I am suggesting that anything physical— including physical entities evolving through the transference and combinations of DNA—represents Infinite Wisdom's expression of creativity and is therefore perfect, related, and unified with everything else. "All religions and increasing numbers of scientists agree that there is but one principle, or consciousness, pervading the entire universe, occupying all space, and essentially the same at every point of its presence" (The Master Key System, Haanel).

Now that you hold a clear picture of where you came from and what you are, you might wonder, what is the source of this vibrational energy? This is the question that, when answered, will assure your passage to a higher level of awareness. What is the basis of everything (including us)? Let's ask American Indian Oglala Sioux, Black Elk:

> Grandfather, Great Spirit, once more behold me on earth and lean to hear my feeble voice. You lived first, and you are older than all need, older than all prayer. All things belong to you-the two-legged, the four legged, the wings of the air, and all green things that live. You have set the powers of the four quarters of the earth to cross each other. You have made me cross the good road, and the road of difficulties, and where they cross, the place is holy. Day in, day out, forevermore, you are the life of things.

Contemplations on the This Second Level of Awareness

Answer the following questions so you may put in your own words your understanding of the concepts discussed above. Your answers represent an important part of the process in your journey into and beyond the second level of awareness. In these truths, you will find the key to accept grace back into your life.

1. How does courage negate our detractors of fear?

    _____
    _____
    _____
    _____
    _____

2. What is the cause of fear?

    _____
    _____
    _____
    _____
    _____

3. What is illusion?

    _____
    _____
    _____
    _____
    _____

4. Identify the thoughts and actions you have that are based on fear.

    _____
    _____
    _____
    _____
    _____

5. Why and how do these "fear thoughts" create your own living hell?

    _____
    _____
    _____
    _____
    _____

Some Thoughts on Transcending Awareness

The result of complete awareness is that you become an outlet for Infinite Wisdom to express itself through the flow of its energy field. This results in abundance, wisdom, harmony, and freedom. Remaining unaware assures poverty, ignorance, discord, and tyranny. And here is the big number-one thought that, if you can accept it, will change everything: Infinite Wisdom (the Big Kahuna) needs you and loves you for serving as a vessel and conduit for its thoughts. You are the channel through which Infinite Wisdom may experience manifestation in this physical arena. You are not powerless. You are not helpless. There is nothing you need. On the contrary, you create all things and all things flow through you.

And now you are ready for the third level of awareness.

CHAPTER 7

THE THIRD LEVEL OF AWARENESS:
LOVE/JOY/GRACE/PEACE

As we move into the third level of awareness, we are faced with one of my favorite contemplations in the entire journey: Is there anything that is not one with everything else? This is not about religion. Any name or theology you attach to the Source represents only an illusionary and incomplete concept of the essential oneness of everything. We could embark upon an in-depth study of that concept, but it would require more space than we could fit into this volume.

Instead, let us begin with this little quandary: Knowing that all of creation has become manifest from the same Source (Infinite Wisdom), why is there such diversity of religions? Why cannot one religion tolerate the others? And why is love, peace, grace, and joy so illusive? Simple: the oneness about which I speak has nothing to do with religion. And religion does not usually lead to the third level of awareness.

Although the world's religions teach love, history reveals exactly the opposite outcome. God is not a building, as in a church or any other structure designed to house a place of gathering for the purpose of worship and fellowship. These places serve a purpose, but they are not God (and you won't necessarily find God there, other than in the matter that constitutes the physical building and the people inside). You may or may not find the essence of God there, so maybe you should keep looking.

Maybe you should just look around you and at yourself. Matter and energy have been shown to be interchangeable. One form becomes the other in a constant flow of energy that originates from Infinite Wisdom. This energy is everywhere in all things, visible and invisible.

So where are you going to find God, Infinite Wisdom, the One? Where are you going to find the Creator or Source Energy? Where are you going to find peace? Science now proclaims that the Source Energy we seek is everywhere because the particles of creation are everywhere.

God Is Not Theology

Theology is a study of religious concepts made up by man for the purpose of directing our thinking and controlling our behavior. Religion accomplishes this goal in a clever way: it lords over us with fear. But fear is not God, Infinite Wisdom. Fear is not love (and make no mistake, Infinite Wisdom is love). Since Infinite Wisdom is love, anything that uses or evokes fear is the opposite of love and therefore should not be included in any theology. This means that Infinite Wisdom isn't going to punish you by placing you into eternal fire. Since Infinite Wisdom is love— pure, unconditional love—there is no judgment, revenge, punishment, or retribution. Infinite Wisdom is not any of these things. These things represent the massive illusionary system of control we know as "the Great Religions."

Bells, whistles, ceremonies, pageants, celebrations, wine, crackers, bread, baptism, robes, pretty buildings, sermons, prayer groups, steeples, pastors, ministers, rabbis, Sunday school, women's groups, tithes, the cross, the star, the crescent moon, symbols, limbo, purgatory—these things are not God, the Creator, Infinite Wisdom. These things are distractions, ridiculous distractions. These things represent the human response to fear and the illusions we have previously discussed.

With this in mind, throughout our efforts to identify and follow natural law, do not think of these things as God, the Creator. If you can do this, you need not view the information contained in this volume as religious. Make no mistake, I love and respect all religions, people, and philosophies and any approach to life based on love. This is the nature of the true human nature stripped free from the detractors. So please, instead of becoming defensive about your own religion, race, or cultural origins, think instead about the state your life and our world is in and what you intend to do about it. Living above the chaos means that we believe we carry with us a power, a natural force, that we can use to follow a better way. The more aware we become, the more love, joy, grace, and peace we are going to experience and share.

Everything is perfect and is as it should be. It took me many years to accept that truth, even though things didn't usually go the way I thought they should. Returning to Dr. Hawkins' Power vs. Force, we learn that "the basic law of the universe is economy. The universe does not waste a single quark; everything serves a purpose and fits into a balance—there are no extraneous events." If we can accept this concept and apply it to our lives, we have taken a large step toward the third level of awareness.

You Are Not the Victim. You Are the Perpetrator.

Hold on now. Let's not get too far ahead of ourselves. If we're going to refute religious principles, we have to first start thinking in religious terms. So let's speculate like those who establish theology. Let's assume for a moment that your soul is more "you" than your physical body. Many religions believe this way. From the East to the West, you'll find billions of people who believe that the physical body is only a temporary vessel for the immortal soul. The idea goes that, while your physical body will change and decay over time, your soul will (ideally) evolve and be around forever. Imagine how you would feel if you really believed this. Maybe you would find yourself dwelling in the energy field of love/peace/grace/joy (the third level of awareness).

Is this just a nice story that makes us feel warm and fuzzy and a part of something bigger and more permanent? Perhaps this belief in the soul as an eternal entity is pure speculation. There is no way for us to know whether our souls exist the moment after we die—and by then, we're not able to tell anyone the truth or the fallacy of the matter.

So when religious principles fail us, where can we turn? Good old science. There's that old law of physics we learned in high school—the one that states, "Matter can neither be created nor destroyed." This obviously can't be entirely true, since all that is came from something created. But at the same time, if it means the sum total of physical creation has already been created, and the sum total of tiny particles is infinite and not capable of being reduced or destroyed, well, in that way, I guess we go on forever.

But since I have no control or real, solid knowledge of what happens after life on Earth or what happened before birth, my only shot at creation is now. So it's up to us to make this life one of love, peace, grace, and joy. And it's up to us right now. So, rather than speculating about the afterlife and killing each other over the argument, let's just all get along. Let's help each other ascend to the third level of awareness.

Let's start with you. You can ascend to the third level and live a life of love/joy/grace/peace. You are here to start feeling better. Acceptance and surrender are part of that process.

How do you describe your life? If you have feelings of lack, bad luck, ill fate or health, or any other "bad" feelings, please consider these as illusions and very temporary. Remember that all things work to enhance the evolutionary process. I know this from analysis of a personal situation that I will relate to you. Infinite Wisdom taught me a grand lesson. I relate it here in hopes that we as one human race can elevate our level of awareness just a tiny notch. Here is my story of a bad situation turning up a most glorious blessing.

My wife was pregnant. I already had two sons and was in the middle of surgical training. This extensive training required five to six years of life dedicated to thirty-six-hour days, call in the hospital every other night, and constant stress and study. The pay was below poverty level. This defines surgical training in the seventies and is why surgeons of that era are grumpy, unhealthy, divorced, and often antisocial.

All I needed was another child. Shocked and devastated, I dropped out of training to take a full-time job in the emergency room. My career as a surgeon was over.

Now fast-forward to the life of my amazing daughter. Yes, I found a way to finish my residency in surgery, and yes, she is an angel. She has always been an inspiration to me and to everyone around her. The world is a better place because of her. She dances professionally in ballet, has two amazing children, a great husband, and continues to spread her joy.

I guess you get the point. But just in case you don't, let me state it more simply: I would die before giving up the experience of my daughter. The situation I thought would ruin my life became a joy and a blessing. This is a common and repeating concept in our lives. If we aspire to the third level, we must accept that we are not always in control and may not always know what is in our own best interest.

The lesson in all of this is that thinking you have a problem (or even a bad life) is pure illusion. It is your perception, belief, attitude, imagination, and closed egocentric mentality that leads you into hell on Earth. Look around you. There are billions of humans on this planet who would gladly take one one-hundredth of what you have and feel more wealth than you could only dream about. So, at the risk of repeating this lesson, learn the illusions and avoid this negativity (repetition is the mother of learning).

This is what I have learned in my life experience. The Universe does not waste energy. Every event or circumstance is not coincidence. The operative term is synchronicity. Complete awareness indicates that all events are related in a symphony of harmonious occurrences that always result in meaning. There are no extraneous events. Don't judge things because you do not have all the facts. Don't try to second-guess Infinite Wisdom. And try to think in terms of the Infinite. All that we see and feel here is only a brief moment in our existence. Quit taking it so seriously. Evolve. Don't worry about anything except making yourself and everyone else feel better. You are the latest version of the greatest vision of Infinite Wisdom. Think about it. This is all the "theology" you need.

Now you have arrived to the third level of awareness, love/joy/grace/peace.

The Burden of Self-Awareness

The laws of the universe are governed by principles of economy and progress. If you believe in Infinite Wisdom, you must admit that this belief must lead you to the conclusion that in fact everything is as it should be. All is well. Otherwise our all-powerful, all-loving God would not be all-powerful and all-loving.

We are capable of arriving at this belief in our conscious evolution because of the awareness of our internal divinity. We are ever becoming that perfect being we originally were. This is the true human condition, free from the illusions and free to express our true nature through unconditional love.

Indeed, there are no extraneous events. We know this because if we were created by an intelligent and loving force, and that this loving force is contained in everything, how cannot everything be perfect? Maybe it's just our perception of things and circumstances that make these things "seem" to be less than perfect. Maybe we do not see the big picture. Maybe we must experience the bad stuff in our lives to gain the maturity and insight required to appreciate the good and to evolve. After all, there must be black for white to exist and cold for hot to exist.

The start of our lives was a miracle (something that significant takes a miracle). If you figure the odds, we really shouldn't even be here. The events and forces required to bring us to this moment and to this place are countless. Yet here we are, with all our baggage—good stuff, bad stuff, and neutral stuff—and, of course, our beliefs. Despite everything that has happened (and indeed perhaps because of it), we are involved in these teachings). You are taking responsibility for your life. This is not a chance occurrence. These events were destined before we even knew of our need.

Your life is the project. It's an ever-expanding, always changing, unpredictable evolutionary journey that you can enjoy.

These perfect events that led us to this time and place began fifteen billion years ago by our illusionary concept of time. At that moment, the elements that constitute the physical portions of our universe were formed. The odds that the shaping and directing of all those things through fifteen billion years of history would lead to the creation of you are (forgive the pun) astronomical. The odds are against it, to say the least. Yet here you are, living and breathing, struggling to survive, to be happy, to understand, and to accept and love yourself.

This struggle has gone on now with our species for, well, maybe several million years. Anthropologists keep moving the time of our birth as a species back. No matter when our species became self-aware, that's when the struggle truly started. Life forms less evolved than man do not experience this struggle. They couldn't care less where they came from, where they are going, or why. These "lesser" life forms are not burdened by the shackles of self-doubt. They are at peace as long as they get enough food and are able to follow their instincts. How ironic, then, that lesser life forms know peace where we typically do not. Remember the cat from our earlier discussion? Look at that cat now. You have been struggling to understand this book while that cat has lived its life instinctively following the concepts you are struggling to understand.

The unfortunate truth is that being self-aware is a terrible burden unless we embrace awareness of our true nature. Lesser life forms do not need to understand or believe. Man, on the other hand, questions, doubts, struggles, and creates chaos from fear. But you know what would put an end to all those struggles? Changing the way, we think about what we have and do not have. It is how we perceive what we have that makes all the difference.

But why and how do we go from the perfect life of our beginning to life as it is now? The answer is simple: we suffer from self-inflicted wounds. This is, as you will see, the way of our civilization. Now don't get me wrong; this isn't a gloom-and-doom exposé on how human civilization and culture is going down the tubes. In fact, it's just the opposite. With this study, we will develop an innate sense that, yes, everything is perfect. WARNING: Even if everything in your life seems perfect right now, get ready, because circumstances are about to change.

The Only Thing Constant Is Change

Change is one of the few things in our lives that we know to be a certainty. The only thing constant is change. As self-aware human beings, we may fight it, or we may embrace it. Embracing change means that we begin to appreciate it, and in essence, take advantage of the opportunities it presents. If we embrace change—or even seek it out as a way to improve our lives—it can be a radical deconstruction of what is and a radical reconstruction of what we want. We have the power to direct the process of change.

Consider yourself at the crossroads. Right now, you're facing radical choices. You can choose to let change happen or you can choose to make it happen. The first step toward grabbing the reins on change is to accept that change does not lead to catastrophe. With the power of change behind us, we can be the creator of our fondest intentions. We can go boldly forward, even if we don't know the exact outcome or destination. We can shake the foundation of our existence and create a new reality. We can emerge from our era of darkness into the light of a new dimension.

Through change, we can discover the latest version of Infinite Wisdom's greatest vision in ourselves. We can possess perfect physical and mental health. We can possess abundant wealth to share freely and wisely. We can grow into perfect relationships. We can find ourselves surrounded by abundance, health, and love. We can have the free will to change and to evolve into an awareness of the enlightened state of being.

Agape Love

By embracing change—thereby transcending our present reality—we now come to learn an advanced new form of love called agape love. We express agape love by being considerate. We give and do not let the object of our affection feel obligated to return that affection. We work toward service, asking, seeking, knocking—and we do it in secret. This is the work that counts. We pay attention and then totally disidentify from conflict while making no attempt to gain attention or approval. We become self-validated. We are liberated from the bondage of conditioning, from complaining, blaming, kowtowing, and accepting authority. This is the essence of the third level of awareness.

As the pure, unconditional love of complete surrender to Infinite Wisdom and acceptance of the perfection of natural law, one's true self emerges and begins to enjoy full awareness. On this level, we experience not only agape love but also self-love. As self-love becomes firmly entrenched into our consciousness, positive energy flows from our beings by way of gratitude, forgiveness, and acts of service. As we dwell in this state of heightened awareness, healing is assured, for once aware we cannot become unaware. Surrender to higher levels of consciousness and acceptance of the present moment become automatic and life altering.

For these reasons, we want to embrace and seek change. We want to evolve into an approach to healing the inner condition (our mental state) through agape love. The outer condition (our physical health) naturally follows.

Through the compelling power of peer pressure, our parents, relatives, friends, education, religion, and culture have taken us from our perfect, blissful infancy to our present state of ego-based thinking and behavior. We are no longer at peace. The pain we perceive as a result has held us back for too long. Let us use it now as motivation to change our perceptions of pain and fear into a drive toward agape love. We can reach that point by discovering, relearning, and appreciating where we came from and what we are.

At the risk of offending your sensibilities, I suggest that if you can't accept that everything is perfect and that you are the latest version of Infinite Wisdom's greatest vision, I'm afraid your journey ends here. At the least, if you can't accept these truths yet, you may need to return to page one and restart your journey (or read the books in the bibliography). Either way, it makes no sense to continue this effort if you don't believe these truths. Make no mistake; you have permission to love yourself, for you are divine. So go ahead and love yourself. And if you can't love yourself just yet, read these pages again and use them to form a new kind of love and appreciation for where you are in your life journey.

If you feel a twinge of disbelief and unworthiness at the thought that you may just be the perfect representation of Infinite Wisdom, you always have the option of going back to your bells, whistles, ceremonies, pageants, celebrations, wine, crackers, bread, baptism, robes, pretty buildings, sermons, groups, steeples, pastors, ministers, rabbis, Sunday school, women's groups, tithes, crucifixes, Stars of David, crescent moons, symbols, limbo, purgatory, hell, and on and on—back to all those theologies and belief structures that got you to where you are today; back to a world of ego-based bigotry and hate. You have free will, after all.

But if you now want to change, motivation to change is the most critical step. It empowers us to take action and get involved. Without motivation, we would never evolve, progress, and improve our communities or ourselves.

My Own Change

Years ago, I reached my own conclusion that if I didn't find a way to change my thoughts and lifestyle, I would soon leave three young children fatherless and penniless. I was in a significant and destructive relationship that involved alcohol and drug addiction. My part in this involved a common response and set of behaviors called code-pendency. I learned that it takes two to perpetuate such a relationship. My efforts of coping included denial and avoidance. Then after months of living in denial, I attended meetings at Al-Anon. It has been reported and widely accepted that the twelve-step program in recovery has helped millions. This may be true, but has anyone ever questioned whether there might be a fundamental flaw to the twelve-step approach? Since its adoption in the late 1930s, millions of addicts (mostly alcoholics) have followed the twelve-steps almost like a religion. Considering the fervor with which so many people follow the program, it really has become something like a cult. But does it work? Yes, it works. For 3 to 10 percent of those who go through the program, yes, it works. For the other 90 percent, however, it does not. It did not and continues not to work for the majority.

And now that I have experienced all of these things, I have come to an understanding of why it doesn't work for 90 percent of addicts or their families. This is my own opinion based on experience and study. To understand why the twelve steps do not work, you need to look no further than the very first step: "We admit that we are powerless over alcohol, that our lives have become unmanageable."

So we are powerless? As the first step in a program that's supposed to empower us to overcome our addictions, we have to admit that we are incapable of managing our own lives?

I tried this approach for several years, and as time went on, I felt worse and worse about my inability to change. I was forty pounds overweight, depressed, and sick. Literally, my life depended on a solid decision to change.

I bring up this story not to highlight the difficulties experienced in my own life. I don't necessarily bring it up to refute the teachings of twelvestep programs either. I bring it up as an illustration for my own need to find change in my life—as an anecdote for how I came to understand the requirements of reaching higher awareness. First and foremost, we must accept change. With that change, we must embrace a new and unfettered love.

As you ponder whether you're ready to ascend to the next level of awareness, ask yourself the following questions:

Do I want to remain powerless over my life?

Have I identified an area in my life that must change?

Do I believe change is possible?

Do I understand the risks involved in avoiding change?

Contemplations on the Third Level of Awareness

1. Do you think Infinite Wisdom (God) cares one little particle whether you call yourself Jewish, Christian, Buddhist, Muslim, agnostic, White, Red, Black, Yellow, Purple, or Green?

    _____

    _____

    _____

    _____

2. Do you know where to find Infinite Wisdom (God)? If so, where?

    _____

    _____

    _____

    _____

3. Do you think you are better or worse than any other person or thing? If so, why?

    _____

    _____

    _____

    _____

4. Are you motivated by pain, pleasure, love, or hate?

    _____

    _____

    _____

5. Do you feel powerless over your circumstances? If so, why?

_____

_____

_____

_____

6. Can you identify or feel pain or discomfort related to your presently perceived situation?

_____

_____

_____

_____

7. How is your misery perfect?

_____

_____

_____

_____

Some Thoughts on Transcending a Higher Level of Awareness

If you're having trouble with the questions above, focus on the concept that everything is perfect. The point, of course, is that if you have a belief system that recognizes God (Infinite Wisdom), you must agree that God is perfect and, just as importantly, that perfect means perfect. Love is perfect, and fear is an illusion. Everything is as it should be. Everything.

If you have doubt that these wisdoms are worth pursuing, imagine a life with no religion for which to live or die. Imagine if we all considered ourselves as one integrated life force. Imagine how you would feel if you could not sin, make mistakes, or need anything or anyone. Imagine a world governed by love, the only emotion not based on an illusion. What would that world look like to you?

CHAPTER 8

THE FOURTH LEVEL OF
AWARENESS: ENLIGHTENMENT

By the time we approach this highest level of awareness, enlightenment, we have already learned that we are different (not better) when compared to other life forms because of our self-awareness. Grace alone granted us this privilege via the process of evolution. The point where the highest level of awareness gets complicated is this: we must recognize that, once we became self-aware, we are faced with the choice of following one of two pathways. These pathways dictate how we think, form relationships, interact with our environment, and interact with one another. Enlightenment means that we instinctively follow natural law.

The first pathway adheres to natural law while the other goes against natural law. The outcome of each pathway is dramatically different. One pathway leads to a thinking process that can be described as disunity while the other as unity. Most likely, your thinking patterns up to now have been subject to the pathway of disunity. This is, after all, the direction our culture shapes us.

It is easy to tell if we are traveling the pathway of disunity. In this case, we find that we play the various games outlined by our culture and society. Because everyone suffers the same discontent that this pathway breeds, nearly everyone else thinks that we are normal for living this way. On the pathway to disunity, we gossip about each other, get caught up in each other's drama, assume each other's addictions, identify with anger, feel jealous, don't like ourselves, allow others to disrespect us, judge each other, and honor the poison of society.

Disunity, or the belief that one thing is different from another, is false, and a false belief can get you into trouble. Such things are the source of all discord in the world today. Remember the God particle? The One? This scientifically proven law of the universe states that everything came from the same source, and so we are all related. No one is better or worse than anyone else. All men are literally created equal. This scientifically proven law of the universe runs contrary to everything upon which we have based our society and culture.

As I wrote earlier, this unity/disunity belief system gives us a choice. There are two pathways, and we can decide which one to follow. At any time, we can reevaluate our belief system and decide to change our pathway and go in another direction.

According to Webster's dictionary, an illusion is "the state or fact of being intellectually deceived or misled." By this logic, the act of thinking in terms of disunity is a false way of thinking. Disunity is separation, and we cannot be separated from our Source, Infinite Wisdom.

When we ascend to the fourth level of awareness, we become fully aware of and in tune with our Source. We start to vibrate with our higher attractor energy field, thereby perceiving things differently. For the first time, we begin to look upon our fellow creation with empathy and true understanding.

Chances are you have never met a person who has attained the highest level of awareness. Would you recognize such a person? Can you imagine a world inhabited by such individuals? Using the information you have found in these writings, imagine that the following ideas apply to you. Design phrases that create your own set of affirmations from the following:

+ The supreme law of life would be love, the power that heals. There would be no fear, hate, or opposition. All life would share a common purpose.

+ Negative detractors would be replaced by positive enhancers. Failure would be redefined as opportunity.

+ Personal success would be measured by the degree to which mankind and all life forms benefit from the quality of the service we render.

+ Imagination (as a projection of Infinite Wisdom) and intuition would be the touchstone of creativity. The impossible would become possible. All doubt would be banished.

+ Mental processes would be acknowledged as cause for all physical entities. Meditation would be the universally accepted method for creating one's destiny.

+ "Now" would be accepted as the only predictor of tomorrow. The past would be seen as the great teacher and motivator.

+ The experience of unity with Infinite Wisdom would be commonplace.

Contemplate the above, using your powers of imagination, and visualize such a world. Now that you understand that you are one with Infinite Wisdom, you may give yourself inspiration to change your perceptions and see truth instead of illusion. If you do this, you will start feeling better. If you do this, you will change the world.

Do you harbor doubt that you can change the world? Consider that you are connected to everything in the universe through the unified field, the matrix of energy that is Infinite Wisdom, the Universal Subconscious Mind. Science has now described and documented such amazing proof of this that it is no longer superstition. Unique phenomena, such as hypnosis (demonstrating the power of the subconscious), psychic phenomena, thought transference, and even reincarnation, taken together all demonstrate the power of the human race to access the energy connections that permeate the universe.

Put these concepts to the test. For the next thirty days, banish negative thoughts and concentrate only on positive, affirmative, loving, and empathetic ideas. You can eliminate the detractors.

Conformity

In Part III of this book, I intend to delve deeply into the concepts of natural law using these reflections in an effort to help you ascend to a higher level of awareness. For now, however, it would behoove us to take a look at the truths that shape natural law.

To those who think in terms of disunity, life rarely seems as hopeful as it is. Disunity has become so commonplace that sometimes it seems that we have forgotten to follow our instincts and feelings.

Reading books, meditating, contemplating, reading more books, and experiencing life should allow us to remember that our instincts and feelings have the power to lead us back to Natural Law and Positive Forces (NLPF).

If you live your life according to NLPF, "You will begin to attract different people and things to you; you are what some people call 'lucky' and things come your way" (The Master Key System, Haanel). You will change your perspective, feel better, and reflect Infinite Wisdom by becoming a conduit of unconditional love.

We know these laws exist because there was a time in our past when we felt no sense of risk. We were not confused; we were on an adventure and were happy and engaged. We responded to the world through true emotion. Then we matured into superficial, emotionless adults. We are not sure what happened to cause this change, but it's likely that we became involved in trying to conform to other people's expectations as to how we should live our lives. We failed to follow our own instincts as to how natural law functions. At the fourth level of awareness, our instincts lead us to follow natural law.

By the time I was a teenager, I had decided to enter the field of medicine. My reason for this was religious in nature. I had learned and believed that Jesus Christ was the Great Physician, and since our church taught that we should try to be Christlike, I decided that I would become a great physician. This is a decision I have never regretted.

The church also taught me that, to go to heaven, I had to be baptized. That meant that I had to be dunked into the water by the pastor. If I failed to do that, I would go to hell. I can remember that this was a scary concept—not just for me, but for the billions of kids throughout the world who didn't know this was so. Were all these kids destined to go to hell simply because they were ignorant of the need for baptism?

Even though I didn't know it yet, this realization summed up the fallacy of religion for me. If you don't do the right stuff, you're going to hell. The entire process is motivation by fear. But isn't God supposed to be infinite love? That's what they told me when I was a kid. So, if He is infinite love, how can He throw you into eternal damnation for not being dunked in a tub of water that sits at the front of the church? When I asked my dad this question, he did not have an answer.

"Dad?" I said. "I'm not as good as God, right?" "Right," he replied.

"Well, I'm obviously not as good and as loving as God, but at the same time, I wouldn't be able to throw that unbaptized puppy there into the fire for even one minute."

"Right," he agreed, somewhat hesitantly.

"Then how can God, who is infinite love, throw people—many people—into eternal fire for not being dunked in the big tub of water at the front of the church?"

Again, my dad didn't have an answer.

Now don't get me wrong; my dad was the best man who ever lived on the planet, but he didn't have all the answers. Dad was brainwashed by religious and cultural teachings. He forgot to think it through. If he had thought about this kind of stuff, he would not have followed the crowd to Sunday school and subsequently he would not have lived his life in fear.

I followed the crowd to Sunday school and was dunked into the water by the pastor in a white robe. For a long time thereafter, I was afraid to follow my own thoughts and convictions. I conformed because I forgot what it was like to be self-directed.

You tell us that baptism is absolutely necessary to go to heaven. If there were a man so good that he never offended God, and if he died without baptism, would he go to hell, never having given any offense to God? If he goes to hell, then God must not love all good people, since He throws one into the fire.

—Young "savage" seminarians to
Jesuit Father Paul Le Jeune, late 1630s

I forgot, and everyone else forgets. It's the herd mentality. I felt comfortable when I looked and acted like everyone else in town. I felt false comfort when I made my family and peers comfortable.

This is, of course, a capsule summary of religion and how it is used to create conformity and stifle independent thinking. This is a microanalysis of what a mess the world is in and why. We conform to the religion and culture into which we are born. Our parents and their parents and their parents decided based on conformity how we would act and what we would believe. This conformity decided whom we would love and whom we would hate. This conformity decided who should live and who should die. This conformity decided where we could live, how we could dress, how we could speak, the definitions of right and wrong, and to whom we prayed and paid homage. This conformity even decided what, when, and how we ate.

Conformity rules. And it is oh so comfortable. This is because it's so much easier to conform than it is to think for ourselves. (And it is even more difficult to meditate, contemplate, analyze, and rebel.)

This is exactly the reason why, as a child, even though I was very much onto something with my line of questioning, I simply stopped questioning. I kept quiet, did what everyone else did, and conformed to a traditional existence. Conformity got me, just like it has gotten you.

Independent, Self-Directed Thought

The most critical component to ascending to the fourth level of aware-ness is accepting our own ability to think independently, no matter how difficult that sort of thing might seem at first. We must do this, for the way we currently live on this earth is far too destructive to be sustainable. Without this higher awareness, we will only continue to inflict wounds upon each other and keep the entire planet in chaos. The enlightened state will have escaped us. Maybe, just maybe, it's time to be non-conformists. Maybe it's time to reject present-day organized religion as ridiculous and dangerous. Maybe it's time to reject our political leaders and organizations that take us down wrong avenues for the wrong reasons. Maybe it's time to reject the Madison Avenue propaganda that controls our thinking and behavior, even what we eat. Maybe it's time to think, time to gain a true perspective in and of our lives.

My research tells me that we can achieve this through indepen-dent, self-directed thought. That's right; it all may just come down to something as simple as thinking with our own minds. Think. Use your head. Wake up. Pay attention. Don't follow the crowd. I recently read that my mind is the mind of God. My conscious mind gives me free will to choose my path. My subconscious mind is subservient to my conscious mind. My subconscious mind is part of Infinite Wisdom. If that is true (and it may be), what follows is true and useful. If it is not true, I invite you to think and decide for yourself what is true.

So far I have learned this: most of our circumstances that we believe are problems actually result from turning our backs on the natural laws that control the universe. Instead, our intention should be to explore the natural laws and discover how we have neglected to follow them. We should allow the time we have left on this planet to be a positive, uplifting experience. We should learn how, just by showing up here on the planet, we have been granted the oppor-tunity of life—and that, if we don't create a good one, it's our own damn fault.

With a higher awareness, if there is knowledge available to apply to this quest, we will find it simply because we believe that everything is perfect. Fear not. Doubt not. Everything is about to get better. Why? Because that is what we want for our children, and we shall come to understand that your children are my children and my children are your children. This may mean that we have to change. We may need to change our perspective and start focusing on who we want to be rather than who we think we are. But it can be done.

"Abraham said, 'In order to effect true positive change in your experience, you must disregard how things are—as well as how others are seeing you—and give more of your attention to the way you prefer things to be'" (The Law of Attraction, Esther and Jerry Hicks). In our case, in order to give more attention to the way we prefer things to be, we must change our self-image from helpless to powerful.

I hope you are not getting confused on this point. To arrive at understanding, you must stop thinking in a conventional way and start thinking as you would if you really believe that you belong to Infinity. If you're not there yet, fake it until you make it. Yes, enjoy each moment of your life here in the form of matter (illusion), but stop sweating the small stuff (and as they say, "It's all small stuff"). As long as you conform to your old habits and beliefs and insane behavior, you are in essence helpless.

What does thinking from the viewpoint of Infinity feel like? It's like clearing the morning fog with the early sun. The fog has no chance against the power of the sun. Helplessness has no power against Infinity. So go there in your imagination, and feel the power of pulling your emotional attachments out and away from the herd. Feel the freedom that self-validation brings to you. Feel the unconditional love that has been granted to you by Infinity. Be a channel for Infinite Wisdom. Meditate and imagine yourself and the entire planet into our ultimate destiny, which is unity.

Our Relationship to Natural Law

Let's recall our conversation on natural law from the introduction. In summary, there are man-made laws that we must follow (at least if we don't wish to pay the price to society), and there are natural laws that we must follow if we don't want to pay the price to ourselves. You can break the laws of society and get away with it. Run a red light, and unless you hit someone or are observed by the police, you will go on your merry way. But natural laws? Break those and they always have a way of coming back to bite you. If you break a natural law, you will surely suffer the consequences. Sometimes that doesn't happen until much later, but make no mistake, it always happens in time.

The other difference between man-made laws and natural laws? If you follow man-made laws, no one rewards you for it. That's just what you're "supposed to do." But if you follow natural laws, you will reap the benefits just as surely as you would reap the consequences if you ignored them.

So again, what are natural laws? The natural laws relate to your mind, body, and relationships. They look like this:

1. Your mind: the natural law is that you must think independent, self-directed thoughts. Use your imagination to think from the infinite state.

2. Your body: the natural law is to nourish your body naturally, respect it, and love it.

3. Your relationships: the natural law is to give what you want without condition. Unconditional love is rare on this planet but try to imagine a relationship based on love that asks nothing in return.

Let's think about these laws in total. They are the only things that matter. And if we can come to accept that, literally all of the other stresses in life fall away. This is the beauty of the fourth level of awareness: it shows us that if we can do just those three things, we will enjoy a wonderfully productive and happy life. We will be able to break the bonds of conformity and allow the herd mentality to melt away. This is living in an enlightened state. Just as importantly, living in this way will help us to improve the world for our children. We can help shape a world motivated by love and not pain and fear. We can become happy, productive, and caring members of society. We can feel better.

Does this seem simple to you? Is it possible that everything that matters can be summarized in three easy-to-follow laws? Absolutely. Following natural law seems simple because it is simple. Moreover, there is nothing more natural than adhering to these laws. We are, in our perfect state, designed to do these things, after all. To follow natural laws really is just a matter of remembering the perfection of who we are. We don't have to learn anything in order to ascend to this level of awareness. We just have to remember who we are and where we came from.

With that in mind, as we attempt to move back to our perfect state in Part III of this book, consider the following reminders. If you follow natural law:

1. your perception of life will drastically improve.
2. you will reconnect with your true self.
3. you will experience self-validation.
4. you will not be controlled by the herd.
5. you will live a longer, more joyful life.
6. your relationships will blossom.
7. you will embrace change.
8. you will be healthy.
9. you will feel better.
10. you will save the world from chaos.

Does any of that sound good to you? Ascending through the four levels of awareness is like opening your eyes (and your mind and your heart) for the first time. It is like the day of your birth, that moment when you first emerged into the world as a perfect human being.

We have already discussed how perfect you are. And now you have learned the path toward natural law and the higher levels of awareness. You have seen and can imagine how wonderful life can be when you live and think this way. Now let's figure out how to make that happen for you!

Contemplations on the Fourth Level of Awareness

1. Describe the levels of awareness.

    _____

    _____

    _____

2. How have the great religions contributed to the chaos on our planet?

    _____

    _____

    _____

3. How have the great religions contributed to peace and joy on our planet?

    _____

    _____

    _____

4. How can you honor and respect your religion and culture and still think independent, self-directed thoughts? (Hint: In infinity, there is no distinction between anything or hierarchy.)

    _____

    _____

    _____

5. Does surrender mean you are helpless or powerful? Why?

    _____

    _____

    _____

6. How does our perspective change when we think from Infinity?

    _____

    _____

    _____

Note: You are required to research and understand all of the previous material to bring together the teachings of this writing. This project is you. I hope you take the time and energy to do the exercises and answer the questions. Many ideas discussed here deviate from your usual perceptions. My goal has been to encourage you to examine your life, accept it as perfect motivation to evolve, and live above the chaos. This is expected if you live according to natural law.

PART III

NATURAL LAW

CHAPTER 9

THE FIRST NATURAL LAW: INDEPENDENT THINKING

The first natural law deals with the mind. Thinking independent, selfdirected thoughts is the natural state of being for all of us.

For centuries, we have believed that the mind is located in the brain and serves to control the body through a network of nerves. This is only partially true. Science now demonstrates that the mind is also connected to the nonlocal intelligence of the universe. Now consider this very carefully. We are one with Infinite Wisdom. Our physical existence in this form is only a shadow of our real selves. The illusion of our mind as equivalent with our brain allows us a functional reference to experience an existence on this vibrational plane. We call it "life on Earth." We call it our "worldly existence." And although we control our thoughts by our intentions and desires (the conscious part of our mind), these thought patterns actually originate from Infinite Wisdom, the Universal Subconscious Mind, as does everything.

The amazing thing is that, through evolution, we have morphed into beings with the ability to direct conscious thought at will. We think with the mind of Infinite Wisdom, and yet we have the free will to control the conscious part of our brains. Our conscious mind becomes the captain of our ship while the subconscious mind draws on the infinite intelligence of the universe.

Let's review what we know so this concept becomes more of a reality in our belief structure. I base the following on ancient teachings, the writings of U. S. Andersen in his book Three Magic Words, and the latest scientific evidence in psychology as well as advanced studies of energy force fields.

1. All that exists—the known worlds, the unknown worlds, matter, energy, both form and formless—functions in a unified field of primal energies.

2. The source of this energy is Infinite Wisdom that cannot be further described, explained, or understood. But we have massive indirect evidence as to its presence. Intuitively, we have learned by experience that we can accept this knowledge and surrender to it (faith).

3. Infinite Wisdom is the Source of energy that fluctuates between energy and form in a continuing flow of life forces.

4. We can understand these vibrational energy forces by comparing a radio transmitter to a radio. Once the frequencies match, the messages come through loud and clear.

5. Infinite Wisdom is the transmitter, and our subconscious mind is the receiver.

We are not presently taking advantage of this phenomenon because we really don't believe it to be real. Our beliefs determine our perspectives, and therefore we are limited by our own self-doubt.

As you know by now, one of the goals of this book is to eliminate that self-doubt. We will do this by remembering not to trust our physical senses because they can only reveal a minute percentage of the truth. The larger truth is that our minds cannot only think but create as well because they are connected to (and indeed constitute) the mind of Infinite Wisdom.

In writing the above paragraph, I recognize that, once again, this might be a difficult concept to accept because most of us have never really considered it. The human condition's default position is to think that because we have never experienced something in our present physical state, we never will experience that something. But we are working toward higher levels of awareness by adhering to natural law. So let's throw out that predetermined line of thinking. Let us instead think in a new way. Let us think and create. Let us think new thoughts. Let us use these capacities to recreate ourselves in our new, highest vision. Let us become the way we want to be and let us do that solely through the creative power of our minds.

We can apply this awareness to achieve anything we desire. "Every condition, circumstance, and manifestation of your life can be changed to suit your conscious desires" (Andersen). The mechanism for this involves the relationship between the conscious and the subconscious minds. The conscious mind creates ideas and images that establish a benchmark concept (desire) for the allpowerful subconscious mind.

How is the subconscious mind all-powerful? It has been shown that although the memory of the conscious mind is relatively short and incomplete, the memory and the power of the subconscious mind is limitless. Experiments in hypnosis and other psychological techniques have demonstrated that memory and knowledge even of past lives are available to the subconscious mind. So, our minds actually function in a dual manner. The conscious mind, while dealing with life as interpreted by the five senses, can create an idea, desire, intention, or goal, and once an intense belief is established (with faith), the subconscious mind (by direct access to Universal Subconscious Mind, or Infinite Wisdom) gets it done. All my research tells me that we do not have to know the "how," we just need to imagine it done and visualize it done. When we believe it, we will see it.

I cannot overemphasize the importance of the relationship between the conscious and subconscious minds. In essence, the conscious mind deals with everything in the material world while the subconscious mind deals in abstract yet infinite probabilities. It is the subconscious mind that brings to fruition what the conscious mind believes.

I saw this concept demonstrated in my own life. And it happened without my even knowing what this process involved. Earlier, I told the story of getting accepted to one of the top medical schools in the country and completing my dream of becoming a surgeon. Truth is, years before that happened, I imagined it, I believed it; it was all I thought about every minute of every day. Every night as I drifted off to sleep, I saw myself as a surgeon. My subconscious mind responded, and in due time, by means I never could have predicted or even considered, I achieved that goal.

Then, in times when I needed guidance—that normally and predictably would have gone badly—it worked again. Remember the young lady who was pronounced dead and yet survived? Remember the surgery I performed, despite not being fully competent in some areas of expertise? I believe that it was my faith, belief, and imagination that pulled from Infinite Wisdom exactly what I needed in order to provide the best care possible.

Here is another amazing incident that kept me on track when everyone was telling me that going to medical school and becoming a surgeon was impossible. One evening, I was sitting in my apartment near the university. I was finishing my third year of college, and my grades were only average. My advisors felt no empathy for me. To them, I was a nuisance because they had experience with average students trying to get into medical school. I decided to drop out, return to my hometown, and reconsider my options. But the powers of the cosmos had another plan.

The evening, the silence was suddenly broken by a loud crash of metal against metal. From my second-story window, I saw below in the street a truck smashed into a metal utility pole. A man lay motionless in the grass with a slowly increasing pool of blood around his head. I ran down the stairs and went immediately to the injured man. His scalp was off his skull and he was bleeding profusely. He was unconscious. I returned the flap of scalp to his skull, wrapped his head securely with my T-shirt, and applied pressure. After an eternity of holding the line against bleeding, the paramedics finally arrived. They pushed me aside and began their work.

I thought about this man for several days. Finally, I went over to University Hospital to inquire about his condition. I flashed my student ID and told them I was a medical student and that I had assisted this man. Finally, I found myself in his room. Once he understood what had happened and that I was the one who had attended to him, he told me that the paramedics had informed him that without immediate care, he would have bled to death. He said, "Thank you so much. You saved my life. You are my angel."

I knew at that moment without a doubt what my life work would be. I had an intention, yes, but it took such an experience to establish a belief. Intention plus belief can dispel doubt. Eliminate the detractors and what is left is pure power.

This is the power of the subconscious mind that you absolutely must open into your awareness. I feel compelled to share this experience. I am not all that religious. I am not a philosopher. I have no special insights. I do not write with a magic spirit pen. I am just a man who has benefited from experience, curiosity, and faith. Consider your own life experience. Chances are you can recall incidents that were initially perceived as negative yet resulted in a positive outcome.

Think about it: What is the alternative? The alternative is continuing to follow the herd—to think about spirituality and science and "what is" and "what isn't" in exactly the same way as the vast majority of people living on this planet. To me, that sounds like a terrible idea. Following the herd is natural for sheep, but we are not sheep. We are capable of self-awareness. It seems logical then that we should be thinking independently, always changing our perspectives and breaking away from the herd mentality.

In case that's not enough motivation for you, consider the fact that the herd is almost always wrong. The herd requires of us that we shun and neglect anyone who doesn't conform. The leaders of the herd will tell you that they know what you should do and think. Sometimes they even claim to know who should live and who should die. What a terrible club to join! And yet we are all members of this club.

Thinking outside the herd takes lots of practice. Everywhere we look and in almost everything we hear, we encounter energies and strategies that tempt us to follow the herd. On top of that, it is more comfortable and much easier to conform than it is to think and act independently. It doesn't help that the "herd people" will often try to frighten us into thinking that, unless we do as they say or "do what everyone else is doing," we'll either be ostracized or worse. If we don't conform to the Christian value system, for example, we'll be tossed into a circle of hell that will torture and burn us and make us suffer beyond description for all eternity, forevermore, and without end. In another part of the world, if you do not subscribe to certain religious beliefs, you will literally lose your head or be tortured to death.

The flipside of this herd propaganda is that if we do what the leaders say we must do, we'll be included in this happy, healthy, and productive existence—or even better, we'll have whatever we want for all eternity, forevermore, and without end. Through this ultimately hollow promise, we can assure ourselves that we will always have enough of whatever we want in order to keep us happy.

The herd mentality stifles our natural instincts to think and understand how the universe really works. And it becomes a paralysis of fear. So, if we hope to adhere to the first natural law, we must first learn a new approach to thinking.

One special note before we move on to discuss how this is done: Thinking in this new way will require quiet. Not only should we quiet the room, but we must also quiet our minds. We must achieve both environmental and mental quiet. Achieving mental quiet isn't easy. It takes practice. Additionally, in this fast-paced world, it is rare indeed to find a place that is truly quiet. It seems there is always a TV, radio, stereo, or computer polluting our quiet time. Even when we go outside, we are often subject to and at the mercy of the roar of traffic. All this noise is unnatural. In fact, we are breaking a natural law simply by not seeking out and allowing ourselves mental tranquility. This isn't a good thing. Remember, after all, that breaking a natural law leads to consequences, eventually but surely. So, as we pursue adherence to this law of the mind, let us attempt to find mental quiet in a quiet environment. Your personal task is to actively seek out a place of tranquility.

The natural laws allow us a direct attachment with Infinite Wisdom. One first controls the conscious mind by active visualization. Visualize your desires as vividly as possible. The subconscious mind then assumes that your visualization is reality, and by tapping into the Universal Subconscious Mind, you will slowly notice a subtle shift in your perceptions. If you persist in your efforts, your vision will become reality. If you have never attempted this before, you are in for a surprise. This is the way of the "natural" in our unnatural environment. Yes, it takes effort, and yes, many factors will conspire to dissuade us, but rest assured that we will reap many great benefits.

Timeout

Let's talk about breathing. When my children were young and misbehaved, we put them in timeout. Usually, this took place in the "naughty corner," but the more I observed my children's behavior before and after time spent in the naughty corner, the more I began to believe that it was improperly named. Perhaps it should have been named the "peace corner." Before my children spent any time in the naughty corner, they would be agitated, angry, hyperkinetic, unsettled, and subject to rapid breathing. After five minutes in the naughty corner, they would be settled, cooperative, slow in their breathing, and happy once more.

Based on this observation, I once decided to put myself in timeout. The first thing to do in timeout is to slow down your breathing. If performed properly, this slow, shallow breathing will slightly decrease the flow of oxygen to your brain cells. Brain cells need oxygen to function properly, and since brain cells allow the function of thinking, what we are trying to reach by slowing our breathing is a state of less conventional thinking. We are attempting to quiet the brain and do less thinking because we have not yet learned to think good thoughts. Further, we have not established a working belief that we can tap into Infinite Wisdom by dictating our desires to our subconscious mind. We are still following the herd and thinking all those negative, self-defeating thoughts. Once we learn to empty our minds of this negative energy, it will be easier to get some good, positive energy flowing in there. Until then, we must breathe slowly and try to quiet our minds.

As we move toward a quiet mind through this slow, shallow breathing technique, our egos will hold onto the belief that thinking requires optimal oxygen flow. But remember, we are not attempting to think for our ego. We are learning to think outside the ego and inside the realm of infinite understanding. This has nothing to do with our physical body's concept of intelligence. It has everything to do with feelings, emotional energy, and a realization of our true nature.

Before we go any further, I have a confession to make. The first time I attempted this exercise, I was very uncomfortable. I wanted to take a deep breath and get the flow of oxygen back into my body, but when I did that, I had to resist the flow of negative thoughts that came with the oxygen. Normal thinking requires oxygen. Without oxygen flow, there is a buildup of carbon dioxide. Too much carbon dioxide creates acid buildup within the blood. This further impedes the normal thought process but also makes it more uncomfortable to continue the exercise. I overcame this hurdle by concentrating on slow, shallow, placid breathing while thinking of nothing else. I willed myself to believe that this was where I wanted to be, this place of ultimate quiet. I told myself that this was a new way of thinking, a way that is less, not more—and certainly different.

In this meditative state, we will consciously ban negative thought.

In Three Magic Words, U. S. Andersen puts forth a challenge. He suggests that if we can ban negativity from our thinking for a thirty-day period, this avoidance of negativity will become a new habit. We will have evolved by using our conscious mind to direct and command the subconscious mind. "The Subconscious Mind does exactly what the Conscious Mind tells it to do."

Negativity. This is the great barrier to awareness. This is an awareness that continually and insidiously contaminates our thought processes. Andersen calls these thoughts "prompters." I call them "detractors." All detractors were placed into our subconscious mind by our conscious mind. Just because the conscious mind is the captain of our ship, that doesn't mean it always acts in our best interest.

Fear is the greatest lock placed on our subconscious mind by our conscious mind. And where did this fear come from? Go back to the introduction. It's all detailed there. Detractors aplenty came from the many environmental influences we have experienced since birth.

That spirit within you is the subconscious mind that is responsive to your conscious mind. And your conscious mind is controlled by your free will to think independent, self-directed thoughts.

Now, before we get too carried away in thinking that I'm asking you to deprive your brain of oxygen every day, just know that I only suggest that you perform this exercise for as long as it takes to eliminate negative thoughts from your daily thinking routine. For me, now that I have learned to replace negative thoughts with positive ones, I no longer feel the need to deprive my brain of oxygen. Slow, controlled breathing, however, assists me in reaching a state of relaxation so as to allow the flow of good, positive thoughts. Your exercise for today is to enter the naughty corner, relax, and use your imagination to visualize your goals and desires as if you are already successful. Do this for thirty days.

One secret to thinking in the naughty corner is how to focus on what we are becoming and not on what we lack. Even as described by Napoleon Hill, according to the laws of attraction, we become what we think about consistently. Notice that I'm not suggesting that we ask for things—only that we think positively in order to have positivity returned to us. Sending out a request or supplication to the universe isn't recommended. It seems that thinking "wanting" thoughts results in "wanting" responses. Think instead of thankfulness for the assurance that Infinite Wisdom wants nothing more than fulfillment for all of creation. Think instead of what you want, focus on it, and imagine that the goal is already reached.

After years of practicing this path toward eliminating my negative thoughts, I have become able to focus my thinking outside the herd mentality. I can concentrate on what I want to be, not what I am. I see myself as becoming good, merciful, compassionate, and understanding. I see peace, joy, and light. I don't care what anyone else thinks. This is my path. I found it. It's mine. And although you can have it too, you can't duplicate it exactly. We each have our own unique paths, and so you have to find your own way. You have to do the work. It's not easy, but it is fun, and for me at least, it has been worth the effort. This has been my reward: I am alive and at peace on planet Earth.

In the past, I thought that meditation was a hoax. I thought, Well, why would I need to meditate when I relax so completely during sleep? To me, meditation was nothing more than a forced sort of half-sleep—and in this way, a complete waste of time. I didn't see it back then, but there's an important distinction between the two. When we are in the deep phase of sleeping each night, we are actually unconscious. We are not aware of our body or ourselves. This is not true during meditation, our own little forced timeout in the naughty corner (or the peace corner). With meditation, we have to actively participate in breath control and focused, slow, positive thought. I have researched several methods of meditation. I found that I was focusing on the method more than the visualization.

My results were excellent once I learned to simply sit down, shut up, relax, and imagine.

This kind of work is what the herd out there is unwilling to do. If you tell someone that you spend some time every day in meditation, they will think you are a religious fanatic. That's how the herd thinks.

Yes, this is real work. It takes at least thirty days of pure determination just to get started. This is another reason that meditation is beyond the herd's ability and willingness to accept. If you find yourself unwilling to make the effort, you can feel free to just return to the herd. It's okay. This isn't failure. It simply means that you need more time to ponder the concept before you eventually return. By then, it will make perfect sense to you. You will wonder what took you so long to break off and find your own wonderful path.

Self-Awareness

Self-awareness is another thing that comes naturally to us perfect beings, but we hardly ever acknowledge it. The sheep in the herd are not self-aware and will discourage any attempts to become self-aware. If you're self-aware, you no longer need the herd, and for some reason, the herd finds this threatening. Perhaps it's because, with self-awareness, you become independent and confident. I think this is something that we all want, and yet the herd frowns upon it.

So how do we get there? Self-awareness can only result from selfanalysis. Notice the "self" in both of those buzz words. I'm not going to analyze you and you're not going to analyze me. Analysis of someone else is just a form of judgment, unless, of course, you're a professional. Your doctor isn't going to analyze you; he can't even analyze himself. Your psychologist can't help you much on this either. He has to concentrate too much on keeping the schedule flowing rather than concentrating on your life problems. This idea may surprise and shock you, but when most health-care providers start the day, they aren't thinking, How can I help someone today? Rather, they're thinking, How can I keep on schedule today? How can I pay the bills? How can I avoid a malpractice lawsuit? How can I get home in time for supper? I'm sorry to say it, but that's the way it is.

Let's talk about your pastor, minister, rabbi, priest, mullah, etc. Given that they've been bought and paid for by the herd, they'll tell you only those things that the herd has determined to be the one and only road to salvation. This road will depend mostly on where you are on the planet and who your parents were. Throughout history, this has also depended on when you were born. Concepts that were taught a hundred years ago are considered pure nonsense now. For instance, the religious groups among us nearly all have long, colorful histories of believing that women can be witches. Today, we believe this to be a purely ridiculous concept. And yet, over the course of civilization, thousands upon thousands of people have died for the crime!

There are smaller ones as well, and they're just as silly. For instance, there was a time when you could assure yourself of salvation by abstaining from eating meat on Fridays. Likewise, you could assure yourself of salvation if someone would buy your way out of limbo. By now, these ideas have been declared void. Times do change; we are evolving, and all is well in the universe.

Self-analysis is what happens in the naughty corner during a timeout. If you're not accomplishing this during your time alone, you're doing something wrong. During self-analysis, you will come to a number of incredible new conclusions about yourself. Often, the first of them is that you are more than your physical body. In fact, you will eventually reach a point where you start remembering that you're mostly not a physical body but rather a consciousness that is merely visiting a physical body during a stop on your sacred journey. This realization is like having the weight of the world lifted from your shoulders.

If you should start thinking of yourself as mostly something other than a physical body, or something in addition to a physical body, what is your true nature? Put simply (and at the same time, not at all simply), you are the center of the universe. The only thing that holds you back from achieving your full potential is your perception and your dogged dedication to your ego-based ideas of disunity.

Consider this: When you find yourself in a state of deep sleep, wreathed in a dark cloud of unconsciousness, where is your nonphysical self then? Your physical body is still there, running on autopilot while your other self is, what? Gone? During this deep-sleep part of your evening, scientists can hook you up to electrical monitors that will measure your brainwaves. There are specific types of brainwaves that can be measured for each phase of sleep. Some of the night, you may exist in a dream state, and sometimes you can remember these dreams. Sometimes these dreams make sense, and sometimes they don't. The point of interest here is that, during all this, the thought processes are apparently separate from the body. The body remains unresponsive while the thoughts (not the mind) can be anywhere, doing anything.

It logically follows, therefore, that your body and your thoughts are two separate entities. We are not just body and mind; we are more. Either we are more or we are connected to something more because the mind while sleeping doesn't consciously create these images; it just transmits them. We don't fall off to sleep and order up a dream sequence. These thought patterns clearly originate from some other source. Is it possible that they originate from Infinite Wisdom? Or is it possible that they come from the universal consciousness into which we all tap?

Here is an interesting question: If the body is the real and only "self," what is the source of sleep dreaming and creative thought during periods of unconsciousness? "This unconsciousness of the body during sleep is an indication that the self is merely a visitant in the house of flesh" (The Secret Path, Dr. Paul Brunton). This is really a radical pronouncement. It gives an entirely new twist to the idea of self-analysis. Before I understood this concept, I thought self-analysis meant to go through and check off a list of things like "I am ambitious," "I am energetic," and "I am friendly." That is all very nice, but it's not the result of the self-analysis about which I write. Once the work is done and we get to a certain point, we understand that the analysis comes down to this: We are more than our physical bodies and personalities. We are connected directly to Infinite Wisdom, and we are immortal.

You may not believe that, but I do. I believe it because I have left the herd, I have done the work, and I am free. I am free from anyone and anything I choose. I am free to embrace the concepts of goodness, mercy, understanding, and compassion. I am free to live in light, peace, and joy.

How does one reach this state? I suggest that by increasing awareness into your true nature, you must conclude that you are perfect.

First define your true nature and then logically follow the steps through the four levels of awareness. If you follow the science and your intuition, this is the only logical conclusion.

Another good reason we do this work is so we may see ourselves through our own eyes and not the eyes of the herd. We become free to see ourselves as we want to be, not as we presently seem to be. Directing and controlling our own thoughts gives us the ability to create. When we achieve the ability to create, we can make the world the way we want it. If we don't make our world, someone else (usually the herd) will. Then we become the victim. Then we will never be free.

Through this process of thinking, self-awareness, and self-analysis, we can recreate ourselves to reach our highest potentials. We can approach what we want to be and abandon what we are (what we think we are).

Mental Entropy

We all want to own and control our lives, but we must overcome at least two problems before we can do that.

The first problem relates to a concept in mental functioning I call "mental entropy." In the study of physics, the term entropy is used to describe a specific property of energy. It is a measure of the uniformity of distribution of energy. This energy can be measured as it is given off during any physical or chemical reaction. If we consider thinking as a physical and chemical reaction, where neurons in the brain react to mental energy, mental entropy functions here as it does in other closed systems.

A good way to visualize how entropy works is to imagine the mental energy as going from localized or organized to becoming dispersed, spread out, or disorganized. It takes work to keep our neurons functioning in an organized fashion. Meditation and quiet time thinking in the naughty corner represents the work that is required to keep mental entropy lined up, organized, and functioning properly. When the work of organizing this entropy is not done, the energies disperse and become disorganized and our mental functions degrade into previously established patterns and bad habits.

The herd mentality has already established most of these bad habits, and so they are deeply entrenched. Mental entropy explains why we must continue our mental work in self-analysis so as to create and maintain new and useful thought patterns or habits. If we don't continually reestablish and maintain mental entropy, we revert to our old mental patterns and bad habits (such as addiction, for example).

The second problem is that we all also seek and need approval, support, and assurance from someone. It started with our parents. Where would we be without their approval, support, and assurance? Lacking that fundamental relationship would make it difficult to eventually reach a level of self-reliance and independence. So, if you didn't get that as a kid, it is going to be more difficult (but not impossible) for you to start not needing these things.

This will be difficult either way, but don't fret. It is essential to get that work done. Essential, that is, if you want to break free and leave the herd. As adults living a so-called independent lifestyle, we shift our need for approval to the herd. As previously stated, that means that the herd controls us. If the herd controls us, it is doing our thinking for us. It's easier to live that way, but the cost is enormous. The herd will tell you who to like and who to dislike. It will tell you who to kill and who to die for. Depending on the herd for approval means we have to dress properly, live in a proper house, drive a proper car, shop at the proper place, eat the proper foods, get fat and sick, consume toxic substances, do crazy things, drive fast, be cool, hang out, use more toxic substances, go to the right church, be religious (or not, depending on what segment of the herd we hang out with), get a good education, get a job, get married, and have a couple of kids and teach them how to be like us—fat, sick, addicted, and "normal."

Contrast this with the concept of owning yourself. Owning yourself means doing none, some, or all of the above, but doing them because that is who you are, not who they are.

So the essence of the natural law about the mind is that we should think our own thoughts and create our own path. We do that by meditation and reestablishing our mental entropy in the naughty corner. We do that by rediscovering our true nature and seeking our own approval and support for the way we want to be.

Who You Are

Should you decide to get involved in self-analysis and eventually tell the herd to get lost, you best figure out who you are—or at least who you want to be. These two things may not be the same at this time, but they can be. Try to think of someone you know who is exactly who they want to be. Do you know someone who is exactly that? Do you know someone who has it all figured out, doesn't want to change a thing, and is happy, content, and at peace? I can't think of a single person who fits the description. It isn't that they don't exist; it's that they are extremely rare.

We are here on the planet to evolve. All of life evolves, and the human race is no exception. I believe we have a choice, though, on which way we want to evolve. We can change in a positive way or we can change in a negative way. Or we can decide not to change anything.

Negative evolution takes place when we fail to follow the natural laws that have been given to us. Since we can think and are self-aware, our evolving is not by chance, nor is it determined by "survival of the fittest."

We evolve in a negative way when we do things and think a certain way because that is the way of the herd. We must open our minds to our own self and seek the highest image we have of that self. We must change in such a way that we raise our standards. With those standards aptly raised, we may move on to improving our outlook on the other two natural laws.

CHAPTER 10

THE SECOND NATURAL LAW: THE HEALTHY BODY

Eight years ago, I experienced the shock of my life. Before that moment, I considered myself to be fairly healthy, although moderately overweight. Like many people who think themselves invincible, I fancied myself as on my way to the lofty ranks of the centurions. But then my fasting blood sugar results came back at 286. The normal optimum blood sugar level is 85. The fasting blood sugar drawn the next day was 307. What that meant was that I had given myself adult-onset type 2 diabetes. It also meant, to my great shock, that I wasn't perfect after all. It meant that I was defective and that I would surely die soon—and in a slow, miserable, painful way, no less. I followed this realization with an immediate bout of depression, hopelessness, and then anger.

How dare this life be so cruel? I thought. I've spent my entire adult life making people well, now here I'm sick and bound to get sicker. It all seemed so unfair. After all, I didn't smoke or consume alcohol. I didn't work out regularly, but I wasn't lazy either.

As it turned out, I was eating too much sugar. This was a rude awakening. As a physician, I had always preached a healthy lifestyle and a common-sense approach to health care. I had advised my patients to eat right, get daily exercise, and lower stress. All this advice I gave out but did not take. In this way, I was breaking a natural law.

I suppose it was in my middle thirties when I developed my terrible eating habits, got too busy to exercise, and, as a general surgeon in solo practice, started experiencing enough stress for ten people. Much of the stress and misfortune I experienced was self-imposed, but the fact remained that I faced too much of it on a daily basis.

As you read this, you might be thinking that something like this could never happen to you. That's exactly the way I used to think. Make no mistake; the detrimental effects associated with a less-than-stellar lifestyle can sneak up on you like a thief in the night. My grandfather would say, "That's going to jump up and bite you in the ass someday," and he was right. Today, we would say that everything we do or even think has consequences. Slowly but surely, your body responds to the inflammatory stimuli that it is exposed to in our modern society. Slowly but surely, all the sugar we ingest, smoke that we inhale, air pollution and sun exposure we encounter, stress we allow, and disease we contract takes its toll on all body systems, from the skin to the pancreas. The combination of these things can lead to a health crisis beyond anything you could ever anticipate.

If you think you are immune to these problems, think again. Unless you have made unusual and heroic efforts to regulate your diet and lifestyle, you are exposing yourself to danger. The average person is usually at least 10 to 20 percent overweight. Many people are much more overweight than that. If you fall into any level of this spectrum, you face grave danger with your health—and probably sooner than you think. Don't wait for your own wake-up call before you make changes in your life.

My health crisis and wake-up call came in the form of an abnormal blood test. I should have known that being thirty pounds overweight and eating all those sugar and fat-laden foods would someday do me in. Unfortunately, I didn't catch myself in time. But once I finally scraped myself out of the depression that the blood test had caused, I knew it was time that I took personal responsibility for my health. It was time to take definitive action. It was time to follow natural law.

As you have probably guessed by now, the second natural law moves the discussion to our bodies. The law states that we must nourish our bodies naturally, respect them, and love them. For many of us, this calls for raising the standards of how we eat, exercise, and otherwise treat our bodies. But how do we go about raising those standards? This is where your new brand of thinking from the first natural law comes into play. Using that thinking, we must first consider all of those things that might be holding us back or causing us problems. It is with these things that we will start our examination of how to apply the second natural law to our lives.

For example, if you are overweight and you want to raise your personal standard to achieve an ideal weight, you have probably been habitually breaking or not following the second natural law. Chances are that you have been eating sugar (in the form of sodas, desserts, and highglycemic carbohydrates), lots of red meat, and perhaps consuming too much alcohol. Also, chances are that you aren't exercising on a regular and consistent basis. It could be that you have gotten into the habit of spending your time doing lazy stuff, like watching television or just hanging out with the herd. Conversely, maybe you have developed some of these habits as a result of trying to compete with the herd. It's tough to eat well and exercise when you're spending ten to twelve hours a day at the office, after all.

Well, these are obviously just a few examples of situations that we must try to overcome if we hope to adhere to the second natural law. This will require some work, certainly, but not doing the work means returning to the herd mentality and not raising our standards. When the work seems hard, take solace in the fact that going down this path is always rewarding because it helps you to realize first who you are and then, just as importantly, who you want to be.

Consider the natural response in our bodies to harmful substances. The response is called inflammation. Inflammation can be a good thing. If an infection occurs in the body, the defense mechanism is inflammation. Certain cells in the body serve to attack the infection and kill it. However, inflammation can run amuck. This happens when too much sugar is ingested or other unnatural foods or substances are encountered (e.g., smoking, alcohol, stress, etc.). Heart disease, high blood pressure, arthritis, lupus, Crohn's disease, Alzheimer's disease, irritable bowel syndrome, colitis, migraines, tendonitis, fatigue, scar tissue, diabetes, kidney failure, and other problems can all be directly related to inflammation.

What causes inflammation? You guessed it, the American diet. Most of what we eat is killing us slowly and painfully. Our food causes inflammation and is lacking antioxidants and other nutrients that prevent inflammation. Sugar and refined white flower have a strong inflammatory effect. Meanwhile, the average American consumes over 160 pounds of sugar and 200 pounds of white flour per year. These increase blood sugar and cause the formation of dangerous chemicals. Sugars cause proteins to cross-link. Then the breakdown of these complexes creates large amounts of inflammatory chemicals.

By consuming sugar, white flour, dairy, meat, and cola drinks, most Americans create an acidity in the bloodstream that results in these disease entities. Most of our fats and oils cause inflammation because they contain excessive omega-6 fatty acids. Omega-3 fatty acids are antiinflammatory. While we should consume equal amounts of these fatty acids, our diets actually contain twenty to thirty times as much omega-6 as omega-3. The bad oils are popular in cooking. These include corn, safflower, sunflower, soy, canola, and peanut oils. Grain-fed beef, poultry, and farmed fish also contain excessive omega-6.

Milk products cause inflammation as well. Dairy cows feed on a diet of grain-containing foods that are very high in omega-6 fatty acids.

Consuming any of the above goes against natural law, and by doing so, we are paying the price. The price is economic hardship and physical suffering (disease).

The New Higher Standard

Let's continue with our example of being overweight because we have not followed the second natural law. Since we want to return to natural law and rehabilitate our fat, lazy bodies (and believe me when I say that I used to have a fat, lazy body), we must set a higher standard for ourselves.

The first step to raising your standards is to start thinking of what you will look and feel like once you have achieved your goals. This visualization is very important because as we discussed way back in Chapter 2, we tend to become the things we think about on a consistent basis. Everything starts with your thoughts. When you woke up this morning, you had a thought. That thought led to action. No matter what you did with that first thought of the day, it's proof that your thoughts are the source of your power.

So, begin by thinking of yourself as lean and in shape. Visualize yourself eating good food and exercising. Then take action. As you take action, keep thinking about how great it feels to be in top physical shape. You look great, feel great, breathe better, and act better. It's a new higher standard.

What does the new higher standard of eating look like? Well, you would be eating very little to no sugar and lots of fresh fruits and vegetables, fish, and low-glycemic index foods and drinking minimal alcohol. You would not be eating red meat. You would be returning to natural foods that are good for you and not riddled with the poisons of sugar and preservatives. You might even get into organic gardening rather than hauling your family off to choke their bodies with fast food. Does this sound like a higher standard to you?

Here we have some simple guidelines: basically, if it falls from a tree, grows out of the ground, or you have to chase it around the forest or get it from an unpolluted stream, you can eat it.

Generally, you can see by the list below that some basic changes in the food you choose can make a huge difference in the inflammation of your body:

1. Eat plenty of fruits and vegetables (raw is better than cooked)
2. No trans-fats
3. More omega-3 fatty acids, as in fish and walnuts
4. No refined or processed foods
5. No sugar

Notice that the emphasis is on natural foods not altered by chemicals or processes that render the foods dangerous.

What would your activity level look like if you set a new higher standard?

We have known for many years that regular, consistent physical activity is the next best thing to a natural diet when it comes to stopping inflammation. It is not important what you do; it's merely important that you do something. Sitting in front of the TV for six hours each day is not one of the "somethings."

Here is what you should do:

1. Set aside each day at least thirty minutes for vigorous exercise.
2. Work up slowly to high-intensity interval training.
3. Do just a little more each session.

Maybe it would be natural for you to walk, jog, swim, bike, or at least do something active that you are not presently doing. Exercising and moving is about raising your standard and keeping to natural law. You will reap great benefits if you do it, and you will pay a price if you don't. As an aside, it has been found that high-intensity interval training is better than long-distance jogging. This concept requires one to exercise at maximum capacity for thirty seconds, working up to one minute, and then recover and rest for one to two minutes. Start with one set and work up to seven or eight sets. Any anaerobic exercise will do, like running, resistance training, biking, or swimming. In ancient times, our ancestors did not run marathons. They survived by adapting to the ability to chase their prey with short bursts of running and dispatching their meal with haste. This type of high-intensity activity has been shown to enhance weight loss and increase muscle mass for up to twenty-four hours after the session. To understand how this works, observe the muscle mass of a sprinter compared to a long-distance runner.

With that working understanding of the new higher standard in place, now we're going to discover how doing this in six important areas of our lives can recreate who we are directly from our vision of who we want to be. First, we will figure out what to do and then we will do what we know we should be doing.

Know What to Do and Then Do What You Know

As we move toward adhering to this natural law, let us consider the areas that may require setting a higher standard:

1. Health: if we are going to evolve, we must feel good physically.

2. Relationships: if we are going to evolve, we must get along.

3. Financial: if we are going to evolve, we must have means.

4. Occupation: if we are going to evolve, we must be productive and of service.

5. Spirituality: if we are going to evolve, we must understand our true nature.

6. Service: if we are going to evolve, we must give back.

This might look like a lot of work, and it might wind up being more than you want to do. If these are the kinds of things you're thinking, I'm sorry to say that you are exactly right. It is a lot of (often difficult) work. What can I say? It will not be an easy task to get rid of that lifetime of negative stuff you're toting around. But you've read the book to this point, so you've already started taking that all-important first critical step. Do the work from here and you will be happy. Don't do the work from here—don't take action to raise any of your standards—and your life will continue just as it is. If your life sucks, that's no way to improve it.

Health: More Than Just the Absence of Disease

Getting up in the middle of the night to go to the bathroom three, four, or five times can be aggravating. It adds to the stress of the day and robs you of sleep. In the morning, you feel like you have worked all night. I lived with that problem for over a year. Then the leg cramps started. Imagine finally entering into a deep sleep, only to be shocked by an unbelievable pain in the lower leg. Imagine jumping out of bed and onto the floor, forced to massage yourself vigorously as you stalk around, trying to relieve your muscle spasms. Then imagine doing all this in between frequent trips to the bathroom.

The funny thing is that I remember my mother complaining of this very same thing for years and years. I remember hearing my father helping her with her leg massage before going off to the bathroom. Now I know what was going on. And guess what? They passed it on to me.

During that same period of my struggle with leg cramps and frequent urination, I noticed that I simply could not get enough to drink. My mouth was constantly dry, and I sought out water wherever I could find it. The other thing I noticed was drying skin on my arms and wrinkles on my neck. People told me I was losing weight. They could see it in my face. All the while, my pants felt tighter around the waist. I wasn't losing weight. I was simply rearranging it.

All these shenanigans slowly took a toll on my energy level. I was tired and grumpy all the time. Little did I know that the worst was yet to come.

The boils that popped up on my face were hideous. On the left side, a row of swollen red pustules appeared on my cheek. I still have a scar where they once were. I consulted a dermatologist friend of mine, and he said, "Hey, so you've got some pimples." Reaching into his medicine cabinet, he fished out a tube of cream and said, "Use this for a week or so and wash your face better."

A month later, I consulted another dermatologist friend of mine due to some more "pimples" on my chin. "Folliculitis," he said. "You must be under some stress." This time, I was gifted some solution from a small sample bottle. "Put this on twice a day and wash your face."

Both highly qualified, board-certified dermatologists gave me topical antibiotics. Two months later, I had another outbreak and met a third dermatologist for an opinion. "It's a boil," she said. She gave me topical steroids and asked if I wanted an injection of the same.

All through this ordeal, I kept wondering whether these doctors were dumb, blind, or both. Am I living in a fantasyland? I wondered. Or should I expect these experts to be asking some important questions here?

In retrospect, they might have asked questions like:

1. Are you urinating frequently?
2. Are you thirsty all the time?
3. Have you noticed increased fatigue?
4. Any weight changes?

And the big, all-important, $100,000 question: Is there any diabetes in your family?

I guess I shouldn't be too upset with these colleagues. I'm a physician, and I was in total denial. Diabetes was not going to get me, I figured. I'm too smart, too savvy, and too cool to let that happen. After watching my parents struggle with multiple bottles of medications, insulin injections, foot and skincare, and all the heartaches of dealing with this condition, I promised myself that I would never get old, sick, fat, and dependent like them.

I was wrong. I was becoming exactly like them, and I had only myself to blame. I had myself to blame for the thirty extra pounds I had carried around for the past twenty years. Too much fat and sugar gave me that typical expanding waistline. Ingesting too much sugar and high-glycemic index foods made me sick. For all that time, I had thought that I was relatively healthy, but slowly I was learning that I had a disease.

Sure, if you have a disease, we can describe you as unhealthy, but just because your disease free doesn't make you healthy. To call ourselves healthy, we want more. We want to crank it up to a new higher standard. As we progress through this chapter, we're going to learn how to be in excellent health—a condition of optimal well-being. What we're talking about here is a rare condition for all too many members of the general population these days. In fact, being unhealthy is so common that it has actually become normal to be obese in this society. It is also becoming the norm to be addicted to alcohol or harmful drugs. (Special note: harmful drugs aren't simply the street drugs you've been warned about; they also can be those drugs your physician prescribes.) In this troubled modern society, the only people who come close to the ideal of health are professional athletes. But then again, with the ubiquitous use of steroids and performance-enhancing drugs, maybe even this group isn't truly healthy.

In any case, it all starts with what you put into your body. The good news is that nature already has provided everything you need. As a rule of thumb, adhering to that new higher standard of health starts with eating naturally occurring foods that haven't been processed and damaged by man. No refined sugar. No sugar-filled candies or sodas. No red meat. No ice-cream. No donuts. Avoid starchy vegetables like potatoes, corn, and carrots (cooked). The only thing you should order from a fast food restaurant is salad, and watch that you don't blow it by adding too much fatty dressing.

But let's not get too wrapped up in the specifics. The food you can eat originates directly from nature. If it is altered, refined, concentrated, and laced with preservatives, don't eat it. It does not require a degree in nutritional science to understand this concept or to make healthy choices.

There is a great deal of concern in professional nutritional circles that even the above-recommended foods do not supply some natural substances in sufficient quantities. This is because (as the explanation goes) the soil is depleted of essential elements that we need for optimal balance. This has created a new industry called dietary supplementation.

Most of the research available points to evidence that can be easily supportive of this concept of supplementation. However, this information usually is popularized by the very same companies that are selling supplements. Nevertheless, some of the evidence is compelling, so the following supplements seem to be in keeping with a natural replacement regime:

1. Fish oil with docosahexaenoic acid (DHA). Omega-3 essential fatty acids.
2. DHEA, an anti-inflammatory hormone that declines as we age. 25–100 mg daily.
3. Nettle leaf. 1,000 mg daily, source of phytochemicals, antiinflammatory.
4. Vitamin E. 400 mg daily, antioxidant, prevention of cardiovascular disease.
5. N-acetyl-cystein (NAC). 600 mg daily, detoxifier of free radicals.
6. Vitamin K. Blood clotting, bone repair.
7. Carnosine. 1,000 mg daily, antioxidant, anti-aging.
8. Probiotics (to improve the balance of essential gut bacteria).

Most physicians tell us to also add a multivitamin to the daily routine. If you adopt the above natural diet and supplements regimen, a multivitamin tablet is probably redundant, but it can't hurt.

Sugar Is Poison

Here's a new idea for you. Think about that concept for a moment. Our planet contains everything we need to live: air, gravity, the elements, food, and water. Is there anything we need that we can't get naturally? What effect would returning to a natural diet have on our health and well-being?

Natural foods would be those foods that grow naturally and are essentially unaltered from their original form. Mankind has managed to negatively alter many of these natural substances, making them unfit for human consumption. Refined sugar is the most important example of this unfortunate fact. Sugar is a substance that, although needed by our bodies for sustaining cellular activity, has been so altered (refined) and misused that it has evolved into one of the most dangerous poisons ever.

Refined sugar is the curse of all animal life forms, especially humankind. If there is evil in the world, it must be sugar. Infinite Wisdom does not create or even recognize evil. Evil is a manifestation of the human condition, perpetrated by man against man. We have free will to create evil or to eliminate it.

This particular evil is everywhere. Sugar is present in almost every man-made food and drink. It is either there in its obvious form or disguised as substances that rapidly convert to sugar during digestion (called high-glycemic index carbohydrates).

These sugars in all their forms do terrible things to our bodies. Highglycemic index foods are just as dangerous as pure sugar, for once these foods enter our digestive tract, they lead to increased secretion of insulin. Sugar-containing foods and high-glycemic index foods (like refined rice and pasta) overstimulate the pancreas to secrete these high levels of insulin. When in excess, this causes energy to be stored as fat. Too much fat leads to obesity. Obesity leads to many health-related issues, including diabetes.

The evil continues. Sugar is a potent inflammatory agent that causes chemical reactions within our bodies. These reactions are literally selfdestructive. The inflammatory changes occur on the cellular level and create what doctors call "free radicals." These substances are toxic to our cells via complex processes that eventually result in premature aging and wrinkling, as well as a long list of degenerative diseases. Diabetes (adult onset, type 2), with all of its complications and associated disease states, is linked directly with the massive consumption of sugar in our diets and the resulting obesity.

Let's explore this concept a little further by following the sequence of events that occurs after ingesting a food or beverage high in sugar content. Refined sugar causes an immediate spike in insulin levels from the pancreas. High insulin levels cause cells to store fat as the aging process is accelerated. There is increased heart disease, cancer, and other inflammatory conditions.

Now I hope you understand why I am describing sugar as evil. Many years of eating foods high in sugar or certain animal fats will add to your weight. If you haven't been exercising during this time, you may be somewhat overweight and may not be aware that your fasting blood sugar levels are out of range. Even a moderate elevation above 125 can be an early warning sign for you. You must be especially vigilant if you have any of the early warning signs.

For instance, we all joke about frequent urination at night after fifty or fifty-five years of age. The media attention is usually on prostate enlargement or cancer, but once those tests are deemed normal, you must keep looking for an explanation. Your physician may not be focused on your list of symptoms or your family health history. This is especially true if you were referred to a urologist. These docs are great at what they do, but their approach will be limited. They may not be taking the holistic viewpoint, and you may go undiagnosed until other more obvious symptoms appear.

Undiagnosed and untreated adult type 2 diabetes can have devastating effects on your health. Every organ of your body will be under attack. You are bound for early death, probably after a miserably expensive medical journey. On the way, your vision will be destroyed and then your circulation. You can literally lose body parts: toes, feet, and legs. These appendages die a little at a time, requiring multiple amputations.

I have seen patients in this situation who were in their fifties, yet when you suggest weight loss, exercise, cessation of smoking, and a healthy lifestyle, they laugh and say, "Right, Doc. Get real!"

All of this relates to a major epidemic raging in this country. This epidemic is killing people at an astonishing rate. It is one thousand times worse than AIDS, much worse than car accidents, and much, much worse than all the wars combined. It is more deadly than influenza, pneumonia, tuberculosis, and all the infectious diseases. This epidemic outkills (and can even cause) cancer. The disease is insidious. It strikes people down in the prime of life and has no respect for race, religion, or financial status. Its effects start slowly and build over time until it is seemingly too late to control. The epidemic is obesity, and sugar and certain fats in the diet cause it.

The epidemic is strengthened by a lack of regular exercise. It is estimated that 1.5 million people die in this country each year from the diseases that directly relate to being overweight. That represents 70 percent of deaths from all causes. This epidemic creates more devastation in our society than all the wars, plagues, famines, and holocausts combined throughout all of history.

A recent study from the Journal of Clinical Nutrition has found that increased consumption of soft drinks and other sugary beverages has significantly contributed to our weight and health problems. In fact, it has been shown that drinking only one can of regular soda per day (assuming an otherwise normal diet) can add an extra fifteen pounds of fat to your body in one year. One soda has ten teaspoons of table sugar per can. Is it any wonder that our children are becoming more obese every year?

And as if that is not enough, consider the new and frightening report from researchers in Sweden. The study followed patients who had slightly elevated blood sugars. These levels were only slightly higher than the normal maximum of 125. After a nine-year study period, the researchers tested the participants for dementia and Alzheimer's and found that the patients in this group had a 70 percent greater risk of developing these mental problems. This means that even mild elevations and moderate overweight problems can have dire consequences in the future.

This study is amazingly significant. Let's just assume that you do all the right stuff. You meditate, study, pray, and free yourself from chemical addiction, but at the same time, you continue to consume mass quantities of sugar (in any of its forms). This study shows that in spite of all your good efforts, you are still frying your brain.

This should serve as a warning to all of us because our health care providers may not be asking the right questions and doing the right tests until it is too late. These conditions should be treated early with preventative measures as I suggest here.

Exercise at a Higher Standard

If you raise your standards of diet to a new higher level, your life will start to rock. If you add daily exercise to your new higher standard, your life will really rock.

You know what to do. You've heard it a thousand times. You have read about it, seen it on TV, discussed it with friends and relatives, and even tried it. You have probably started your exercise program many times before stopping. Sometimes it's because you are feeling lazy. Sometimes it's because you aren't sufficiently motivated. Sometimes you are inconsistent with your efforts. Even if you read an article about creating a sexy new you, every time you see one—and even if you follow the advice for a couple of days—it's entirely possible to run out of motivation and go back to the herd mentality right when things start getting tough.

If you see anything about yourself in any of these descriptions, you might want to go back to the naughty corner and do some self-analysis. Ask yourself again about who you are and what you want to be.

You know what to do, now do what you know. Concentrate more on who you want to be. Visualize it and convince yourself that you are already there. You are not going to get help from anyone. This is a selfhelp program, after all. You reap the benefits and you pay the price with hard work.

It's possible that you may not be ready for all this work. If you aren't ready, you will return to the herd until you "hit bottom," as they like to say in AA. Hitting bottom is when you wake up one day and say to yourself, "Enough is enough already." It may be a slight insult from a friend. Maybe someone says something like "Have you picked up some weight recently?" Or it could be the day you realize you have to purchase two airline tickets just to fit in those cramped seats. I hit bottom when my blood sugar test came back at over three hundred. However, you get there, once you hit bottom, your emotions will kick in.

Be thankful because that is the moment of your redemption. Getting emotional about anything is a sure way to make progress.

Fortunately, hitting bottom and getting emotional isn't the only motivator if you're having trouble getting started. Psychologists have determined that the only thing that motivates stronger than emotion is the pain versus pleasure relationship. As a rule, we humans seek pleasure and avoid pain. This accounts for most of what we do. So, in other words, in order to make this kind of change, the pain of being unhealthy has to outweigh the pleasure of eating poison foods, taking drugs, or simply being lazy. Pain versus pleasure. Once you understand this relationship, you can know that you can accomplish anything that you associate with pleasure—even if you may have to endure pain to get there. Some types of pain are easy to endure if you believe it will eventually lead to pleasure. Exercise is a prime example.

It takes courage, insight, determination, and consistency to get results from an exercise program.

While I intend to share some insights about exercise in the coming pages, this is not going to be a fitness guide. You know what you should be doing. You should be moving, using your muscles, walking, jogging, playing games, aerobics, lifting weights, doing a tiny bit more each day until you reach a fitness level that makes you feel good. And for your own sake, be consistent.

Consistent, progressive daily exercise is exactly what it takes to follow the second natural law, and you know very well by now that following natural law leads to great benefits.

The cosmos in general and this planet specifically function to allow our physical bodies to exist, thrive, and relate. A strong, healthy body is a natural thing. Our miraculous bodies need water, oxygen, trace elements and minerals, food, and movement. These things we have been given. We have everything we need. We may not have everything we want, but it is in the wanting that we have created for ourselves a confused, dangerous existence. Maybe it's that we want too much or that we want things that are not good for us.

When we take too much of the right things, or even a little of the wrong things, we disrespect the natural law that controls our healthy physical (and mental) bodies. Knowing and keeping the natural laws can make all the difference in how we look and feel. Looking and feeling well can make all the difference in any area of existence. So, it is very important to respect the laws.

Any thought, deed, or intention that does not honor your body is akin to treating the second natural law with disrespect. For now, in this field of existence, remember this most important of lessons: Break a natural law and you will suffer the consequences (eventually, but surely). Follow a natural law and you will reap great benefits (eventually, but surely).

The Core Values of the Second Natural Law

Don't let your health slip away from you. Prevention is critical. It makes so much sense to start now. Eventually, you will have to adapt these concepts anyway, so you might as well start as soon as possible. Start today!

"Start how?" you ask. It's simple. First, stop making excuses. It's so easy to say, "I can't start now because I am too busy." Wrong. You can, should, and must start now, today, no matter what your schedule looks like.

How can I make such a bold claim? Because adhering to the second natural law is unbelievably simple. How simple? All it takes is these four things:

1. Eat only the foods that your higher self tells you are healthy (hint: you may want to start by eliminating sugar from your diet).
2. Eat reasonable quantities of food.
3. Exercise more today than you did yesterday, even if it's just one more step.
4. Chill. Relax. Help someone else.

The thing to remember as you try to get yourself attuned to the second natural law is that you can't get caught up in the "too" syndrome: too much, too little, too late. Too much sugar, too little natural foods (or exercise), too late to fix your bad habits. Don't make excuses, and don't conform to this poor lifestyle just because it's part of the cultural norm.

That last piece of advice is especially critical in these times in which we live. We've gotten to the point where it's so easy to come up with an excuse to justify just about anything. But think of it this way: an excuse is just another way of lying to yourself. After all, the basis of an excuse is not reality. Here are some examples:

"I can't lose weight because ..."

"I can't exercise because ..."

"I can't stop smoking because ..."

"I can't stop drinking because ..."

You can fill in the space after the "because" with just about any excuse you can imagine. And you know what? It doesn't matter what phrase you use because it will be a lie. If you eat the right kinds and quantities of food and get the proper exercise, you will lose weight and your body will return to a healthy state. In many cases, this will render your excuses moot.

When you say, "I can't lose weight," this is one of the worst lies you can tell yourself. The reality is that you are simply not willing to do what it takes to lose weight. Since you are not willing to pay the price to achieve your goal, saying, "I won't lose weight" is much closer to the truth than saying, "I can't lose weight."

If you adhere to the second natural law and demand a higher standard from yourself instead of living the lie, you'll be living the dream. Remember our discussion about thinking making it so? The same applies here. Your thoughts set the standard for how you live your life. You can choose to live the lie or the dream, and it is all up to you. I choose to think healthy thoughts, and you should too. Project yourself on a screen inside your mind and see yourself healthy, vibrant, and sexy. Do this, put in the work, and before you know it, you'll look exactly like that picture you have in your head right now.

Sometimes this first step of committing to losing weight or living healthier can be the most difficult. There are just so many apparently viable excuses at hand. So instead of stating an excuse, ask, "How can I?" Once you ask that question, the more mature and committed part of you will step out of its shell and seek an answer. Be aware, however, that you will not reach an answer until you have the courage to ask the question.

So now that you know you cannot make excuses, get started on restoring yourself to health once more. You will be pleasantly surprised to see how well your body responds when you start doing the right things. Whenever you feel yourself slipping away from your new lifestyle, remind yourself that even a small amount of excess weight and moderate sugar use can put you at higher risk for future health problems. It can also negatively impact your ability to achieve balance and harmony in your everyday life.

With respect to healthy living, balance means achieving a favorable relationship between what you eat and what you do. If you consume too many calories and too much sugar and fat, and do nothing to increase your metabolism via exercise, you are going to be unbalanced. You will wind up breaking the second natural law. And more than likely, you will get sick as a result.

For years, I chose to make these same mistakes. That ended for me when I received the wake-up call of diabetes. I'm happy to report that now that I have been following the second natural law more closely, I have lost a tremendous amount of weight, feel substantially happier, and have my diabetes under control.

So as you think about your future, you have a choice to make. Either you can continue making excuses about the health decisions you have made or you can keep to natural law and reap the benefits.

CHAPTER 11

THE THIRD NATURAL LAW: RELATIONSHIP

The third natural law gets us closer to the Source by extending the peace and happiness we have found for ourselves into the relationships we form with others. Here the natural law calls for us to give what we want without condition.

Do you know why it is often so difficult for us to formulate completely harmonious relationships? In a word: fear. But what are we afraid of? Are we afraid we might be rejected? Are we afraid that our love isn't good enough? Are we afraid that every relationship will end in pain?

The kicker here is that this can be a self-perpetuating cycle. Fear causes us to lose love and a lack of love tends to produce more fear. "The only remedy for lack of love is perfect love" (A Course in Miracles, Helen Schucman). We first experienced relationship-related fear during the domestication that came about in our formative years. We felt fear of abandonment, fear of not pleasing our caretakers, and fear of conditional love. We discovered that if we did the right things according to our caretakers, we received that love, but if we did the wrong things, we were punished or corrected.

Infinite Wisdom is pure light and pure unconditional love. Since we didn't experience this love as children, we are now seemingly unable to practice, give, or receive unconditional love. Fortunately, as a physical manifestation of pure light, we are in fact capable of unconditional love. It is indeed the ultimate source of peace and joy.

If you are serious about achieving this new level of awareness, I suggest that you send these thoughts out into the cosmos so that Infinite Wisdom may resonate with you. These thoughts are designed to negate your ego and settle your mind into a new and higher awareness of spirituality.

1. Choose to be easygoing and forgiving.
2. Focus on unselfish service and respect to all creatures.
3. Avoid negativity. Replace detractors with positive enhancers.
4. Seek to understand rather than to condemn.
5. Trust in love, mercy, Infinite Wisdom, and compassion.

If you are used to praying regularly, keep in mind that if you follow the above steps, you need pray but one prayer. This prayer will apply to any situation, anytime: "Let me proceed without error to achieve whatever is best for all."

This is the only prayer that resonates with Infinite Wisdom for one simple reason: we do not know what is best in any given situation. We may think we know what we want, but we don't know what's best. We cannot possibly have all the facts, so how could we ever know what is the best outcome?

The only choice is to accept and pray the only prayer that works: "Let me proceed without error to achieve whatever is best for all."

Whatever Is Best in Relationships

We are nothing without our relationships. In my experience, I always have been amazed to witness how a bad relationship can stifle one's creativity, attitude, self-assurance, and subsequent love of life. Indeed, this book began in direct response to my efforts to survive relationships and keep families intact.

The relationships about which I speak did not survive. Fortunately, the ex-wives, the children, and I have survived, and we are all doing well. This happened by the grace of God alone. But for a long time, I have been living in fear that if I begin a new relationship, this will all happen again—a fear that I am somehow destined to live and remain addicted to chaos.

When I refer to my transformation in the matter of relationships, I always call it "the project" because this moniker suggests that the journey will never be complete. How could it ever be complete when we know with certainty that all things are impermanent? We keep evolving and things never remain unchanged or even completely predictable. But there are certain natural laws that, once we master in awareness, allow us to evolve with less suffering—and that is surely a good thing.

Every relationship we analyze will have problem areas. There always seems to be some sort of trust issue. This ranges from trusting that the other will be faithful to trusting in a feeling that each will continue to do what is required to help the other. Can there be a relationship where each says to the other, "As you wish," and truly means it? Can there be a level of trust that "knows" that what you wish is what I wish? Further, is there ever the possibility that, in all our relationships, we can maintain composure and clarity? Can we mean what we say and say what we mean? Can we stop the mind games and be happy instead of insisting that we are right all the time?

Let's try an experiment. Let's make a couple of assumptions and apply them to our very close relationships.

> Assumption #1: We are never going to agree on everything. We have different backgrounds, different experiences, different childhoods, and therefore different points of reference.

Assumption #2: I cannot have adequate knowledge of everything you have ever experienced, and therefore I cannot judge you, correct you, or disagree in any way. We live in two different orbits.

Assumption #3: We understand and appreciate our different reference points, and therefore we must love each other without condition. Loving you doesn't mean I control you. Loving you is a decision I have made, so I want you to remain in my life.

Assumption #4: We live in two different orbits because of our different experiences, different backgrounds, and even different hormones, but that doesn't mean we can't agree to disagree. Sometimes our orbits will be in sync and we will agree. Sometimes we may not agree, but we may compromise.

Thinking about the above assumptions, we begin to see what a good relationship looks like. It looks like trust, composure, clarity, wakefulness, and truth, and if all of that exists, we have freedom, love, and respect. All of this gives us a great chance at a good relationship.

Relationships can falter and even fail because of the inherent differences between male and female physiology. It's like the two genders come from different planets and thus function in different orbits. Recently, writings have explored the connections between mind, body, hormones, and behavior. So, if you want to understand why men and women think and act differently, and thus often encounter difficult relationship issues, you must consider the physiology of these dynamics as well as the personalities.

For now, however, the bottom line is that the knowledge of the four assumptions will give us a full understanding of how unconditional love, trust, honesty, and respect are essential in any successful relationship.

The New Higher Standard

Just as we set a new higher standard in our diet and exercise regimens, we must also seek to set a new higher standard in our relationships. To exist happily and harmoniously with the rest of the world, we need relationships. And this is the case with literally everything in life. For example, absent a reader, what would be the point of writing this book? We are nothing without our relationships, and yet, strangely enough, we spend little time and effort enhancing our most important relationships.

For the most part, we tend to think about our relationships as vehicles through which we might obtain something. We ask ourselves things like "What reasons do I have for staying in this relationship?" and "What am I getting out of this relationship?" If you're asking these kinds of questions about any of your relationships, those relationships are probably going to either fail or make more than one person very unhappy.

So let us take our relationships to a new level. Let us create a new higher standard by asking another question. That question? "What can I give to this relationship?" You see what I did there? Shifting the focus from what you will receive to what you can give represents adherence to the third natural law and brings you one step closer to the positive force that is Infinite Wisdom. The law here is simple: give what you want to receive. If you want a great relationship with someone, give love, respect, power, help, and empathy. Take it to a new level and this natural law will have you experiencing the deepest and most rewarding relationship you could ever imagine.

The best part? By giving you always receive. The new higher standard in your relationships will help you change and evolve into who you want to be.

The Joy-Pain Cycle

Many years ago, I read a book by Paul Davies called The Mind of God. It wasn't a religious or spiritual book. Rather, it was steeped in physics. To my satisfaction, at least, despite its scientific basis, the book described God, the origin of life, and the makings of the physical world. It also described the nonphysical world in physical terms.

I bring up this book here because it raised an important question for me at the time: if we can explain the nonphysical world with physical terms, can we then understand why we feel the way we feel? Can we finally understand the sources and usefulness of our conscious minds and thus our behaviors? And does it explain why and how we feel differently at different times and why this waxing and waning of feeling is usually unpredictable? If it is unpredictable, is it also uncontrollable? In hard times, can we control the ego-based inclination to feel pain? In good times, can we control the ego-based inclination to feel joy? I ask these questions because if our joy depends on some external requirement (like a relationship), a requirement that eventually and inevitably will vanish, we thus establish conditions for our next perception of pain. In this way, the cycle continues and our misery expands: joy-pain-joy-pain-joy-painjoy-pain.

Please consider the above very carefully. Awareness (complete awareness) of this concept can change everything in your reality and certainly in your relationships. It's worth repeating: if joy depends on some external requirement, a requirement that eventually and inevitably will vanish, we thus establish conditions for our next perception of pain.

For example, Sue seemed happy and well-adjusted. I asked her if she had had a joyous Christmas this year. "Absolutely not," she said. I fell into her trap by asking, "Why not?" It took her about twenty minutes to describe her family situation, the comings and goings of relatives, people showing up who were not expected to show up, people not showing up who were expected to show up, poor attitudes, problems, family infighting, gossip, and on and on it went. She was depressed and obviously in pain because Christmas didn't turn out the way she had wanted. And the family relationships were in danger.

You can see how Sue based her joy at Christmas on external events, people, and things. For this reason, she had no control over any of it. So she now feels pain, not joy. As I analyze this example in more depth, I see that the joy she experienced during some previous Christmases established a benchmark that could not be duplicated—so in reality, her previous joy established conditions for her present pain. If she's not careful, the cycle will continue to repeat itself each and every Christmas until Sue changes her perspective through awareness and simply accepts people, situations, and things as they are. This is especially true of her family and intimate relationships.

The question becomes, can we accept our friends, loved ones, and relatives as they are without judgment? The answer is of course yes, provided that it is joy and peace we desire and can accept these things without judgment.

On a practical level, those things over which we have no control we might just as well accept anyway. The control issue is one of those beliefs that, once you make a quantum leap into higher awareness, becomes an erroneous concept. It may be that when we achieve awareness, in many situations we understand that we didn't cause it, can't cure it, and can't control it. In this way, we must simply accept it. For example, you're never going to change or control your in-laws. You can either let them continue to cause you pain or you can accept them and love them for creating your spouse. Likewise, you are never going to change your son or daughter-in-law, so you can accept them and love him or her for choosing your offspring.

Joy or pain. The choice is up to you.

There Is Never Enough Money

One of the most frequent points of fracture in any relationship (particularly of the romantic variety) is the question of finances. There is never enough money is the way the thinking goes. If this is how you're thinking, my friend, you are wrong. There is plenty of money; you just haven't figured out how to get control of more. Having financial freedom and independence is mostly a state of mind. Well, not really. In reality, it's more like a state of fiscal responsibility. Don't spend more than what you make. Save a little.

One of the central points to natural law is that a life that consumes more than it has given doesn't prosper. Life in that situation cannot evolve, and so it perishes. Attracting more money into your life is not going to happen as long as you are constantly thinking about how much money you don't have. The universe does not respond to "wanting." It responds only to "allowing."

Money. Let's talk about money. No, let's talk about abundance. Money is just an instrument we use to assure security and abundance. As physical beings living in a world of competition and perceived scarcity, most of us are concerned about a new house, a new car, nice clothes, taking care of our families, insurance, etc., and when we have enough, it is never enough. Yet studies have shown that we need an approximate equivalent income of $50,000 to feel secure and relatively happy. Anything above that figure does not actually add to happiness. This explains why we see so many unhappy wealthy people.

"What if something happens to me? What if I get old and sick or lose my job?" These are the concerns of the raven. We need security. And the raven teaches us that anything not of the material world does not exist. If I don't have a large bank account or sound investments, abundance does not exist. And then when I reach these goals, it is never enough and I have to worry about losing it all.

But wait. I'm going to make you aware of something. It's something I consider miraculous. It's even better than that. I'm going to relate an unbelievable concept first defined by Neville in The Law and the Promise. Neville describes the law (another natural law) of such magical qualities that you may question the applicability of this law to your own personal life situation. I assume that you will trust me on this one because after I explain the law as I understand it, I will testify through my own experimentation how this magical law took my financial status from day-to-day survival to an abundance that seemed impossible.

It's the law of reverse transformation. I am quite certain that unless you have studied the works of Neville, you have never encountered or considered this law. We see one example of the law if we consider the mechanical action of speech. A mechanical action through any means that creates a sound is nothing more than vibrational energy detected by mechanical means in our ears. We hear these sounds. One day, a very clever man considered the possibility of inverse transformation—that is, reproduction of speech from mechanical motion; thus the phonograph. Another example is the production of electricity from friction (the electric generator). Then we discovered the opposite—that electricity could in turn produce friction (an electrical engine).

Now for a metaphysical explanation:

> Whether or not a man succeeds in reversing a force, he knows, nevertheless, that all transformations of force are reversible ... This law is of the highest importance, because it enables you to foresee the inverse transformation once the direct transformation is verified. If you would know how you would feel were you to realize your objective, then inversely, you would know what state you could realize were you to awaken in yourself such feeling.

In other words, believe you already possess your goal, and you will.

There are several assumptions we must consider to clarify this metaphysical law of reverse transformation. They are as follows:

1. Everything is pure energy. The vibrational frequency of that energy determines the state of the object or entity. Solid objects actually vibrate at lower frequencies. These energies are detected by our five senses.

2. Consciousness precedes matter. Nothing exists first as a physical entity. It first exists as pure vibrational energy. This realm exists outside our five senses. This fact does not mean it is not real. This realm is the only reality.

3. As physical entities of Infinite Wisdom, as the latest version of the consciousness of IW, we possess the exact preeminent

consciousness that creates the content and quality of our lives. Our thoughts and beliefs create our world.

4. Through the power of visualization and imagination, we transform pure universal energy into material manifestation.

The great cycle of Infinite Wisdom is from energy to matter and back to energy. The law of reverse transformation is active in our lives based on awareness of these concepts and belief. You are now aware, but you lack the belief. This is the paradox of the human condition. You believe only in the raven. You doubt the power, nay, even the existence of the dove. The raven is illusion while the dove is truth. Truth always prevails. Foster this belief and practice visualizing your desires. Neville taught that this is accomplished only through self-directed thought in a meditative state. So put yourself in the naughty corner and convert your guilt to pure desire.

My own personal evolution into a belief in the power of the dove started in early childhood. Our family was not poor. We had all we needed to live a fairly comfortable life. Although my father's income was often less than ideal, it was adequate to give us security, shelter, nourishment, and comfort. Yet it gave us nothing beyond necessity. My parents lived through the Great Depression and, as a result, existed in a kind of poverty consciousness. They believed in scarcity and deprivation because this was what they had experienced even as they labored hard to succeed. And they taught that same poverty consciousness to their children. If I had twenty-five cents to spend for lunch, I felt guilty using that money for food, and never would I attempt to buy something extra. Any change I would dutifully return to Mom.

Guilt is a worthless emotion in this setting. Even as an adult, I felt guilt anytime I did anything special for myself (a rare event). And yet, as my world expanded, I noticed others having what I wanted. My desires began to overpower my guilt. Unknowingly, I began to use the powers of reverse transformation. I would go to the hills above our town, look down on the small village, and visualize myself as successful in every respect. I saw myself in nice clothes, driving a car, living as a scholar student at State University, and becoming a surgeon. I had no plan—just a vivid imagination. And it all happened just the way I imagined it.

Your exercise is to put the power of reverse transformation to work for you. It takes imagination in a meditative environment and a strong intent. Recall a less-than-ideal situation in your life and reverse it in your subconscious mind by imagining a perfect outcome.

I no longer feel guilty about my successes. I know that this is what Infinite Wisdom expects of us all. The Universe expands and evolves through our desires ... with one single caveat: we are to do no harm to any other sentient being. Our desires and dreams come to fruition at the proper time, when we are ready, and Infinite Wisdom leads us there if only we surrender our desire. And imagine vividly the desired outcome. Neville said, "What would be good for you? Tell me, because in the end, every conflict will resolve itself as the world is simply mirroring the being you are assuming that you are."

So now we see the importance of our own self-concept. In this awareness, we must assume the very best of ourselves ... and then once we pass into our desired state, we continue to evolve. Soon, we become saturated with abundance, feel secure and comfortable, and then by another miracle of transformation, turn our attention to the dove. One may even wonder what all the suffering and stress was about in the first place. All spiritual traditions of the world teach us this: "One cannot renounce what one has not attained. To move beyond the material world, or its wealth, one must know that wealth." In essence, this explains why happiness really does not expand much after that magic $50,000 figure. Once survival is assured, we innately seek the influence of the dove.

Your Occupation

The new higher standard for your occupation requires passion. If you wake up each morning dreading your shift in the "salt mine," you eventually will not wake up. You will stumble through your life in the zombie state of misery. I know this state because I lived there for several years. Teaching high school chemistry, physics, and biology is certainly a worthy profession. And I enjoyed it, but it was not my passion. I faked it for a while, but the security of a nice position, respect in the community, and accomplishment somehow left me empty and unfulfilled. I was willing to lower my own standard for a paycheck.

Eventually, it caused me such discomfort that I had to do something. In this case, my pain led to avoidance. I went to see my doctor in the hopes that he would write me a prescription for my migraine headaches. I thought it would get rid of the pain and help me keep my secure position. I was wrong. He was wise to tell me something I needed to hear. He told me to never give up on my dream. He said that all the pills in the world would not solve my problem. He looked at me with empathy and compassion. I imagine he experienced these same obstacles in his own life, coming from Italy and speaking no English. He said if he did it, I could do it. Once again, I unknowingly experienced the amazing insight defined by one word: grace. I left his office with no prescription, but my concept of what was possible was elevated.

What I gained that day was not the vision. I already had the vision. What I gained was enthusiasm for the vision. What I gained from a wise soul was validation and belief. I now understand this process. Our purpose is to succeed, perhaps against all odds, and then to pass that energy on to another. Our energy of desire, imagination, vision, enthusiasm, and empathy is the universal energy that drives the evolution of the universe. And we maintain this flow by positively encouraging others in our sphere of influence. If you have never experienced such grace, imagine it and you will. Trust me. It's not a secret body of unobtainable knowledge.

You just gained awareness. Stop feeling sorry for yourself and get your ass in gear!

The Core Values of the Third Natural Law

As you embark upon your journey of accepting the third natural law, it helps to keep in mind a series of core values that can and should shape your perspectives, set your priorities, secure your parameters, clarify your purpose, and focus your pursuits. There are seven core values, and at the risk of repeating my previous teachings, study this list:

1. Infinite Wisdom is the energy field that permeates everything.
2. We possess the power of Infinite Wisdom within us.
3. We can use our imagination and intuition to access the Infinite Power of the universe.
4. The vastness of Infinity teaches us that anything is possible.
5. As individuals created from Source Energy, we are all one thing, and therefore there can be peace.
6. We are perfect beings because of our Source.
7. We save the world from egomania by sharing this message.

In keeping with the above core values, we position ourselves to control our own destiny. In other words, with these tenets in hand, we may choose the time and degree of our awareness. Achieving the highest level of awareness can happen now—right now—or we can wait a year, ten years, twenty years, or even an entire lifetime before we allow it to happen. If we wait long enough, we will not have to work for it, for it will be given at the moment of moving from the physical to nonphysical realm (some think of this as death). By then, we will have missed out on a lot of fun, adventure, and the joy of helping others.

For this reason, choosing to reach a higher level of awareness now is a good idea. Choosing now will enhance the evolutionary progression of our species. Tapping into the way of Infinite Wisdom through the teachings can help, for we seek here to clear it all up and make it easy to awaken into self-awareness, abundance, good health, wellbeing, vitality, sobriety, and, yes, power. Interestingly, if we hope to adhere to the third natural law, that power requires of us something we might not initially expect: it requires that we serve.

Service

One of the most important requirements for adhering to the third natural law is that we must give and help as much as we can. If you have not given something and/or helped someone today, you have broken natural law. It is difficult, after all, to maintain a high level of self-worth or selflove when all you do is take.

> Serve the needs of others, And all your own needs will be fulfilled. Through selfless action, fulfillment is attained.
>
> —Tao Te Ching, 7th Verse

As you can see from the above, this is not a new idea that I'm promoting here. The Tao Te Ching was written almost three thousand years ago. Verse seven speaks of a philosophy that, when followed, has the potential to transform your life. Everything we do naturally is self-serving. When we serve ourselves by taking all we can get and spending for the things we don't yet have, we serve ourselves poorly because the natural way of the earth and universe is to give and serve. It's a true paradox that serving others serves ourselves, but we can easily put this concept to the test.

Try this: give this shift in your thinking a thirty-day trial run. For thirty days, help and give as much as you can in your relationships, occupation, and especially to your family. You will be utterly amazed at how things will change in that brief time. If you like it, keep doing it.

CHAPTER 12

POINT OF DECISION

You stand at a crossroads in your life. The decision you make will advance your life performance, and by keeping within the natural laws, you will attain a higher level of awareness and reap the benefits, eventually and surely. It will require work, and it will mean taking on increased responsibility, but with that work and responsibility, you will have earned new privileges. These privileges will release you from the herd mentality and allow you to live your own life instead of the life prescribed to you by others. If you hesitate now and remain in the world you know, it will require less work, but you will continue to live as a taker instead of a giver and be less independent and less productive.

This is your point of decision. Now is the time when you will ultimately decide if your life will rock or suck.

With your levels of awareness in mind and the natural laws at hand, I'm happy to tell you that there is a large number of life's "greatest" questions that you no longer have to worry about pondering. They are the kinds of questions that everyone everywhere has asked at some point in their lives—it's just that, for most of these people, when they asked them, they didn't yet have the tools to see how irrelevant the questions truly are. Consider the following:

> Where does the universe begin and end?
>
> Why does it exist? Is there a God, and if so, why?
>
> Why is there hate and discontent?
>
> Why can't we all just get along?
>
> What happens to us after death?
>
> Does reincarnation exist?
>
> If so, how does it work?
>
> Who are these holy men called Jesus, Buddha, Mohammad, etc.?
>
> What is the point to all of this?
>
> Why do we evolve?
>
> Why is there pain, suffering, addiction, and on and on?
>
> Why do our behaviors lead to broken relationships and broken families?
>
> Why can't I give and receive unconditional love?
>
> Why can't I feel secure?
>
> What am I afraid of?
>
> Will I ever get straightforward, no-bullshit answers to my questions?
>
> Are there answers that I can depend on, no matter what?

As you know by now, this book does not seek to answer any of these questions directly. These questions are part of the great mystery. But complete awareness and subsequent acceptance of natural law will render all of these questions and any others you may have about life and the universe completely and utterly irrelevant.

I am very happy for you as you stand on this precipice of your new level of awareness. You have all the knowledge you need to start down the path toward your own quantum insight. A quantum insight occurs as the level of awareness increases from the zombie state of "normal" consciousness to an awakened state of understanding. If everyone can find a way to achieve this same quantum insight, the "normal" (and insane) world we know will eventually evolve into a world of beings who have achieved awareness. This is the next step in our evolutionary process, one that we must all strive to encourage.

Please do not take this next idea as in any way disrespectful to the divinity and remarkable teachings of those mentioned. But while pondering the state of our present evolutionary status, with all the negative thinking we have locked into our subconscious minds, what would we be if we were treated since infancy as, say, Christ or the Dali Lama? We consider these savants as divine, wise, compassionate, and even directly descended from God. My theory is this: How special would we feel if we were treated, taught, respected, and honored like Christ or the Dali Lama? Didn't Christ say that we are his brothers and sisters and that we are capable of all things of which he was capable? Do we have any reason to doubt these teachings? Are we innately capable of radiating the "Christ Consciousness?" I think the Dali Lama believes he is special because this is what he was taught.

Conversely, what do we teach our children? What would the world look like if we taught our children in such a special way? Since Christ said what he said, I believe that the next big step in our journey to total awareness is to be accomplished in this way: teach children unconditional love. How do we do that? Love them unconditionally.

Whenever I make claims like the above, people ask me how I can be so confident in this next step in our evolution when there is so much suffering in the world. I usually answer this question with a question of my own: Why do we suffer in this material world? As far as I can tell, there seems to be five reasons, all of them correctable, the result of our own choosing, and linked to our tendency to conform to habitual behaviors. They are as follows:

1. We suffer because we do not know our true nature.

   What is your true nature? One might answer this question by describing what one does for a living or where one comes from. One might respond by saying one's name. As you have learned from the insights provided in this book, these common concepts of self are mere illusions. Once you discover your true self, you will put an end to your own suffering. And once we practice unconditional love, there is the end of suffering.

2. We suffer because we identify with the ego, our sense of separateness from everyone else.

   Once we became domesticated as children, we bought into the belief system that says we are separate and therefore vulnerable. The process of domestication helps us survive in society, but at a great price. The price is our constant feeling of not being and not having enough. We can never be good enough, smart enough, or have enough. We suffer as a result.

3. We suffer because we cling to that which is transient and unreal.

   Once we achieve financial stability or stability in a relationship, we discover how very difficult it is to maintain the status quo. This is because there is in reality no status quo. So, don't waste your time trying to maintain it. If we identify with the transient and unreal, we are destined to suffer as these things slowly but surely slip through our fingers.

4. We suffer because we fear.

   Since we eventually learn that nothing is permanent, we begin to fear loss of that which is ultimately and assuredly going to change. Our fear of change—the only true constant in the universe—assures our suffering.

5. We suffer because we dread death.

   Yes, the greatest fear is that everything that is our self is going to die. Everything will be lost in death. We fear there is nothing good in the afterlife—or worse, that we will suffer in the after-life for the things we did or did not do.

Fortunately, now that you are aware of the tenets of this book, you recognize how and why all of these sources for suffering don't have to be relevant so long as we don't allow them to be. We can put an end to suffering through our awareness of the reasons and possible solutions for these self-inflicted wounds. Think about these responses to the five sources of suffering:

1. We suffer because we do not know our true nature.

   Our true nature is the physical manifestation of the perfect consciousness that is Infinite Wisdom. We are in fact the latest version of the greatest vision of Infinite Wisdom.

2. We suffer because we identify with the ego, our sense of separateness from everyone else.

   Overemphasis on the ego assures that our experience in this physical world will include suffering. Instead, we can balance our ego with an inner awareness of the true nature of our infinite state.

3. We suffer because we cling to that which is transient and unreal.

   Overemphasis on material things, possessions, success, youth, accomplishment, and wealth can be replaced by balancing our lives with awareness of the infinite state of our true nature.

4. We suffer because we fear.

   There is no need to fear loss of that which we do not actually possess. We truly don't own anything so we have nothing to lose. Replace fear with surrender, acceptance, and love. Begin to trust Infinite Wisdom instead.

5. We suffer because we dread death.

   We dread death when we forget our true nature. There is no death in the awareness of our infinite consciousness.

This book describes a process of investigating the science that can reveal natural law. Natural law, when understood and experienced fully, can end all suffering. There is an underlying unity to all things. Integrating these beliefs and teachings is sometimes difficult because our understanding is fundamentally an individual process. It is rarely transferable from one person to another. And it is intuitive, residing above the realm of the intellect.

In awareness, we may experience a "knowing" of natural law. We possess an innate understanding of this due to our connection with Infinite Wisdom. The task is to remember this wisdom. We can remember our innate wisdom by detaching from our ego-oriented nature.

The teachers and sages of natural law are restricted to no particular group, race, or origin. Awareness means that we recognize the value and truth of all the sages and teachers, and we do so with complete awareness. We accept everything as an important part of the way to adhere to natural law and do as Infinite Wisdom intended for us to do.

The only thing that matters is discovering a new perspective, one that will lead you on your way to a higher level of awareness. Aligning old wisdoms with your new understandings is an excellent way to get to the heart of the truth, but it also requires your sincere desire to evolve—and it requires work too.

We must understand that we are not yet fully aligned with natural law and may never be. There will remain times when our lives seem disjointed and confused, but each day, they will become less so. And now that we can perceive things differently, we know that everything fits together perfectly as we become more aware of the real world.

Through awareness, we will create a new reality. Once aware, no matter what we do with the information, our lives can never be the same. But if we reach awareness and then acceptance, we can perceive this new reality and rediscover our true nature, a nature based on love instead of fear.

All of our lives are minor variations on the same theme. This is because we entered this physical existence perfect in every way, but by age three or four, we were brainwashed, manipulated, and domesticated. We have learned from our society certain perspectives that have created the world we see now.

Know this: that which we have accepted as the normal human experience is in reality an ever-changing unnatural state of insanity. Even widely accepted science is often proven totally false. The world is no longer flat, witches no longer exist, and we won't go to hell for eating meat on Friday. The old concepts explaining physics and mathematics have been replaced by quantum concepts that put into question our ideas of causation and consciousness. And what we're finding is truly exciting. What we're finding is that we're no longer powerless over our peace and joy.

Over the years, we have learned very important concepts of survival and integration into a society based on fear. The degree to which we live in fear is related to what we experienced in our local and early environments. The beginning of our egos was the beginning of our fear. In A New Earth, Eckhart Tolle describes the ego as a "primordial error of misperception." In other words, it's just another illusion.

The way you dissolve this illusion is to be aware that it is an illusion. It's a process of disidentification. All those ideas and concepts, possessions, beliefs, and opinions must be seen as what they are: illusions. They are not real; they are not you. This is just more defective software mistakenly downloaded into your otherwise perfect hard drive. This ego illusion is the result of the conditioning of your past.

Anytime you experience anger and defensiveness, it may be a symptom of the ego defining who you are. Attachment to anything signals major ego involvement. "Sometimes letting these things go is an act of greater power than defending or hanging on" (Tolle). It's okay to be proud of what you accomplish (or have), just be conscious of and detached from assuming that these things define you. One way of letting go of attachment and yet continuing to function as a well-adjusted, relaxed, and productive citizen is through the awareness of surrender.

Our journey into awareness will lead us to one startling conclusion: all things, circumstances, and occurrences are perfect just the way they are. Oh yes, I know; this can be a difficult thing to accept in this chaotic and often fearful world in which we live. But this is only because you have not achieved complete awareness ... yet.

The study we have completed, the life experiences we have been blessed with (good and bad), and the people we have had the privilege of knowing (some positive, some negative) have compelled us now to significantly increase our level of awareness. You are invited to join this project and contribute to its evolution. By working together in the project, we are counting on you to help make a difference. The project exists only for the enhancement of our journey together through the eternal process of personal growth and service to others.

If we seek answers, we must first ask the right questions. The project seeks to ask the appropriate questions. We trust in the wisdom of our collective consciousness to reveal answers. But once revealed, it falls to each individual on the planet to act on this information. Achieving complete awareness renders all further conflict mercifully unnecessary.

The original mother of this effort was desperation and need—and pain. Yes, pain is sometimes a useful motivator, but it is never the best one. It isn't the ultimate motivator. Love is better. This is the ultimate message. Love, or more specifically, unconditional love, can stop any pain.

Previous to this awareness, we (perhaps like you) didn't know where we were going as we agonized over not ever getting there. There was no peace, contentment, or trust, only fleeting joy. But our awareness facilitates an awakening to some enhanced understanding that will be useful to anyone who takes the time and has a need.

I suspect that at this very moment as you read or hear these words, your ego is beginning to control your thought processes. This occurs in two ways. Either it doesn't allow your mind to focus enough to fully comprehend this message, or out of suppressed fear it places these thoughts in the category of "pure bullshit." Both reactions occur on the subconscious level and block any real desire to continue in awareness. When your superego kicks in, you find yourself consumed by guilt, anxiety, and feelings of inferiority. In this state of existence, you then need to activate your defense mechanisms. Your life returns to its state of devotion to denial, displacement, intellectualization, fantasy, compensation, projection, rationalization, and reaction formation.

Snap out of it! Think it through. We are slave to our fears—fears just like the defense mechanisms listed above. This is a direct result of our domestication in childhood. Fear is the root cause of all the "reality" we choose to perceive in our lives, and we perpetuate it through our interactions and relationships. "Fear is the source of disease, of war, and of alienation from the joy that is our birthright" (Don Miguel Ruiz).

And why is joy our birthright? Because joy and love is all that really exists. Everything other than joy and love is unreal, an illusion. This concept represents the essence of awareness. The sole purpose of this book is to guide you step by step into this new reality.

Your ego will fight hard to maintain a hold on your misconceptions of reality and how you should relate to your environment. But don't let it. If you find yourself letting it, ask yourself these questions:

> Am I happy and content in my ego-based existence? Am I who I want to be when I look in the mirror?
>
> Can I continue doing what I am doing and expect to get a different result?
>
> Am I willing to read, think, gain awareness, accept, take action, share, and serve?

I hope you answered "no," "no," "no," and "yes!"

Of course, these answers may make sense to your intellect up to a certain point. That point brings you to a wall that exists between your present self-concept and your new awareness. This wall stops the process in its tracks. The only way through this wall of ignorance is your imagination.

> O, let your strong imagination turn The great wheel backward, until Troy unburn

—J. C. Squire

We can turn the wheel backward. We can revise the past by using our imagination and visualization. As noted, we are the products of our domestication and past experiences. Can you imagine how different your core beliefs would be if you were encouraged more, praised more, loved more, nurtured more, and handled difficult moments and decisions differently? Your self-esteem would be greater, you would have more confidence, and your present life would be different—possibly even better.

> Let us put our minds together and see what kind of life we can make for our children.

—Sitting Bull

RANDOM SUMMARIZING THOUGHTS

Fortunately, as awareness expands, our level of consciousness also increases. This creates a major shift in our attitudes and beliefs. That which seems real at one level seems utterly ridiculous at another. You may notice that, as awareness advances, negative concepts no longer control your thoughts.

Life can be compared to a walk on the beach. As you walk on the beach, you leave evidence of your passage as footsteps in the sand. Some of these footsteps might be errant, like the mistakes you have made in your life. But your passage overall can follow one determined path. And the best part is, even the errant footsteps eventually get erased by the Source that is the ocean.

So it is in life. The closer I walk to Source (Infinite Wisdom), the faster and more completely my past gets erased and I can focus on the present. The further I walk from the Source, the longer it takes to restore the "beach" of my life to its pure, unchanged, natural state.

The original intent for this writing was to document evidence that my research had uncovered and to leave something of value to my children. Maybe they could benefit from my experiences. I suspect that my experiences are not much different from or more significant than most, except through pure grace, I have survived a number of situations that led me to question everything. I even questioned the reasons why I might want to remain in this life of chaos and disappointment.

Experiencing situations that should have led to physical injury or even death, essentially without a scratch, and then failing to live up to my own standards is perplexing. There was the rollover in my car into the Ohio River, being buried in a twelve-foot hole on a construction site, talking down a berserk marine who wanted to shoot anything that moved, and then being told by a valued colleague that I was a walking dead man. I burned through failed marriages, producing nine children, two bankruptcies, and a surgical career that became so demanding that my spirit was depleted. I was floating in a quagmire of confusion and perceived failure.

I immersed myself into every self-help book I could find, but I could never answer my own questions. On the exterior, I looked successful and was functioning on a high level of service to humanity. I was a good father.

Because of early childhood experiences and religion, I carried a set of unreasonable fears. I feared death. I feared God. To avoid hell, I tried and failed to emulate the life of Christ.

Judging one's self as a failure (in anything) is an illusion. Yet the experience of failure can have far-reaching effects and is perceived as real. It's so real to us that we react in very negative ways.

My energy decreased and I had no interest in anything. There was a prevailing sense of hopelessness that could at times only be relieved by eating bad food, in large quantities. I stayed in bed for as long as I could. I wanted nothing to do with friends or even family. I felt that I had no love to give or to share. As these feelings surfaced, I felt no ambition to improve my surroundings or myself. I wallowed in self-pity as I became less and less healthy. I could sit for hours staring into space, seeing nothing.

All of this was a misperception of reality, for as my awareness of Infinite Wisdom increased, I eventually accepted my failures as an important, even essential gift.

I experienced the revelation of unconditional love at the Pyramid of the Sun, when I was forced to view the world from a different perspective. The view of the world through the eyes of love, surrender, and acceptance made me feel better. I felt bad, and now I feel better.

The teachings in this book are ever-expanding and ever-evolving consciousness. Yes, we are all perfect, even in our perceived weaknesses and unawareness. These perceptions give us a feeling of negativity and thus suffering. But we arrive at a point that motivates us to rethink our position. Suffering in any way is a signal that we are not aware of the perfection and divine nature of all things. Having a concept of the God particle, that eminent power that constitutes Infinity, we may now perceive all things as manifestations of pure, enduring love energy. With or without somebody of scientific proof or intelligent explanation, we define these feelings as true, simply because it makes us feel better.

How may we define and understand awareness? The following list has been compiled from many different sources. However, a belief in Infinite Wisdom means a belief that all concepts and all of creation originate from that one Source. So actually, this list comes from many sources, yet one Source, Infinite Wisdom. The list is in no particular order and by its very nature is incomplete. You should add to this list. This is the new twelve-step program! We all need this because we are all addicted to chaos and an insane world we define as "normal." We are "chaosoholics". And it is not anonymous; we cannot hide from this condition.

1. Awareness: the source of experiencing

    In our experience, we do not evolve unless we awake from our zombie existence and understand that all we perceive with our five senses is pure illusion. Our concepts of what is right/ wrong, acceptable/unacceptable, good/bad, real/unreal, all fade into oblivion as we open our awareness into the truth. Experiencing without awareness is not to experience at all. It is reacting, but not creating and not evolving.

2. Awareness: requires suspension of previous belief systems

    We believe what we believe because we have accepted false-
    hoods as truths. We have adopted the false person and called
    it conformity. This is based on nothing more significant than
    where we were born and raised, our culture. We had nothing to
    do with this, yet it dictates who should live and who should die.
    Walking into awareness would require a complete reevaluation
    of what we believe as truth.

3. Awareness: the realization that all suffering stems from the
    illusion of individuality.

    In our illusionary world of form, we honor the individual as
    free to encounter the environment, make choices, and com-
    pete. Our success is often at the expense of someone else. And
    after we win the victory, we suffer to maintain that for which
    we have fought. But wait, we all came from the same source, we
    are all related, and if we surrender to the concept of uncondi-
    tional love, all this conflict settles as a raging river is calmed by
    the ocean.

4. Awareness: everything is perfect and nothing needs to be done.

    We are of Infinity so we have the capacity to view our lives from
    the infinite perspective. We (the finite) cannot improve on
    perfection.

5. Awareness: our Source is Infinite Wisdom. The love from Infi-
    nite Wisdom is unconditional, immutable, given in grace, and
    cannot be earned or manipulated.

6. Awareness: all entities and nonentities are equal. There is no
    hierarchy of importance.

    Nothing is superior; nothing is inferior. The entire cosmos is
    one unified thing.

7. Awareness: accepting things as a child. It is what it is.

    All things are given with equal grace. There is no good/bad or
    right/wrong.

8. Awareness: surrender

    Surrender to Infinity as we did at conception, in utero, and will at physical death. Do it now.

9. Awareness: we cannot know what to do.

    We can create an outcome, but we have no ability to devise the proper means ... except in our imagination. Why? Because we do not know all the facts. We cannot possibly know.

10. Awareness: all things work for good; synchronicity

    All entities and events are determined by Infinite Wisdom.

11. Awareness: our purpose is to transmit the light. We do this with happiness and unconditional love.

12. Awareness: your intent assures your evolution. Imagination reflects your intent.

    Evolution starts in your imagination.

My life is better now than it was. From the perspective of Infinity, just like every other manifestation of the universe, my life is perfect. But from my own perspective as a human being, it seems that it is not. Yes, I feel better, but an innate settled feeling of perfection sometimes continues to escape me. I am aware of new and exciting concepts, but my life remains a project. I continue to be addicted to chaos. I have not avoided the news of the day; the human drama that plays out on a daily basis intrigues me still. I struggle every time someone offers me some wonderful sugar-laden treat. I say "no, thank you," but it is a struggle, and sometimes I enjoy ice cream. There is this one person whom I have only initially forgiven, no matter how I try. Life is a project. Not a struggle, not a test, and not predictable, but an evolving project.

Yet, I feel better, and since striking out on this vision quest, I have increased my level of awareness. I have eliminated many of the detractors and negative thoughts from my conscious and my subconscious minds but not all of them. Every day I set an intention to have a great day, do no harm, and help someone. It simply feels good to think in this way. I still have back pain and leg cramps at night, and I still wake up at three

a.m. and wonder if the conflict in the Middle East is going to finally ignite the world into WWIII, but now I can accept these problems as perfect evolutionary events. Another thing I noticed is that a good sense of humor helps. Probably the two most important traits in an aware person are surrender and a sense of humor.

I still experience conflict. Awareness does not mean utopia. The chaos will always be with us. Becoming aware of certain natural laws can help us live above that chaos. Surrender and keep your sense of humor.

I have not invented this way of thinking, but I have been blessed with just the right amount of suffering to become motivated. I thought about the cave. We all have a "cave" in one form or another. It could be work, drugs and alcohol, food, sex, gossip, hate, bigotry, or suicide. I learned that the cave is an option, but not one that was going to make me feel better. If we consider all the caves, we find that ultimately we feel worse ... until just the right moment. This moment may be at physical death, or by intention it could be now. If we choose now, we have time to feel better and pass that feeling on to another.

I have compiled information from many different sources. In some cases, I cannot accurately define these sources or even defend all the decisions I have made along the way. Yet in awareness, I understand one thing. All these sources and decisions point in the same direction:

Love governs all and love is the supreme law of life.

It starts with love of self. Love yourself because you are the latest version of God's greatest vision. Just look around you. What you see is what you created. It all came from your thoughts and your imagination. Control this and you control your total destiny. And the other amazing awareness is that nothing around you is as blessed as you. You have selfawareness, life experience, creativity, empathy, potential, ambition, energy, imagination, and, best of all, you have the capacity for unconditional love. You possess all this because you are the latest version of God's greatest vision. And your heart, kidneys, lungs, bladder, brain, intellect, and imagination are working—flawlessly.

This gives us a moment in infinity to realize our destiny. Our destiny is to evolve. As individuals, we can evolve into a perspective of interconnectedness. We are already connected, yet we perceive separateness as a part of the grand illusion that is the world of form. We evolve through awareness.

The ultimate purpose of life is to be happy. Yes, our species evolves, but the important evolution is that of the consciousness. The physical evolution responds to survival pressures in the environment (external) while our evolution of awareness responds by setting our intention (internal). We influence this form of evolution by controlling our thoughts. We can, with positive intention and imagination, raise our level of awareness and eventually evolve to complete unity with Infinite Wisdom. We will give the raven less and less attention as time goes on. But life here and now is meant to be joyful. We will enjoy the perspective of the raven and surrender to the dove and do no harm.

Let us all do this now because it seems more like a true existence. It feels better to be optimistic, it feels good to forgive, and it feels good to love unconditionally. Setting this intention is increasing our personal standards. Increasing our personal standards in several key areas gives us mental peace. Good health and well-being cannot proceed from a corrupt mind. And mental confusion ultimately leads to disease. Not following natural law leads to an unnatural state of disease. It leads to insanity. If aware, we recognize our "normal" existence as pure insanity. But we are aware. We know a truth that sets us free.

We transcend our detractors by recognizing them as useless negativity, and we feel gratitude for this insightful awareness.

You there, reading and thinking, hear my advice. Go into your imagination and use your creativity and sense of humor to elevate your level of awareness and attract positive energy into your perception. Do this by learning and by living the following affirmation.

Final Affirmation: Infinity

My Source is Infinite Wisdom. I believe that everything is perfect. All perceived imperfections are illusions. All negative thought is a result of my domestication. I am alive and healthy. I believe I always have been.

My survival is never threatened because I belong to Infinity.

I believe that as a being of Infinity, I am not restricted to the narrow perceptions of sight, smell, sound, taste, or touch. I believe that I have the power of imagination and intuition to create my life as the latest version of God's greatest vision. I can serve others by sharing this vision of perfection. I accomplish this by banishing all doubt and negative thinking. I can love unconditionally, recognizing that everyone does the best they can within their personal level of awareness. I believe that through the practice of unconditional love, I can forgive any transgression. I believe in the connectedness of all life forms as one integrated consciousness that emanates from Infinite Wisdom. I can imagine into existence peace, joy, love, reason, acceptance, and courage. I believe the world can change by rediscovering true nature as the latest version of God's greatest vision. I honor and follow natural law.

The illusions of insanity that seemingly permeate this world become important tools in the ascent of my personal journey into awareness. Therefore, I feel gratitude for all things and I accept all things as perfect. Infinite Wisdom is perfection.

We are finished here. It is time for you to take your newly discovered awareness to the world. It is time for you to start feeling better. It is time for you to manifest yourself into that person you know you are: the latest version of God's greatest vision. You are perfect.

THE NATURAL LAWS OF CONSCIOUSNESS

1. Everything is perfect. You are exactly perfect.

2. Your true nature is nothing less than the concrete manifestation of the energy of Infinite Wisdom, the Creator of all things.

3. Love yourself, everyone, and everything without condition.

4. Peace and joy are yours through surrender to Infinite Wisdom.

5. Balance your ego with intent to serve.

6. Your consistent thoughts become your destiny. Consciousness precedes matter.

7. In this world of form, everything changes.

8. Engage in action as dictated by your imagination and intention and then detach from the results.

9. Imagination and intention consistently held in consciousness assures results, but he who accepts these gifts and gives nothing back is a thief (Krishna).

10. Everything you need is provided in a natural form.

11. Every circumstance or experience is perfectly orchestrated to assure your evolution.

12. Your purpose is to evolve and be happy.

BIBLIOGRAPHY

Andersen, U. S. Three Magic Words. Chatsworth: Wilshire, 1954.

Braden, Gregg. The Divine Matrix: Bridging Time, Space, Miracles, and Belief. New York: Hay House, 2007.

Chopra, Deepak. Power Freedom and Grace. San Rafael: Amber-Allan, 2006.

Gandhi, Mahatma. Gandhi's Way to God. New York: MJF, 2009.

Goswami, Amit. God Is Not Dead. Charlottesville: Hampton Roads, 2008.

Gray, John. Venus on Fire, Mars on Ice. Coquitlam: Mind, 2010. Haanel, Charles F. The Master Key System. New York: Atria, 2008. Hawkins, David R. Power vs. Force. Carlsbad: Hay House, 2007.

Hicks, Esther and Jerry. The Law of Attraction. Carlsbad: Hay House, 2006.

Hicks, Esther and Jerry. The Astonishing Power of Emotions. Carlsbad: Hay House, 2008.

Hill, Napoleon. The Law of Success. Chatsworth: Wilshire, facsimile edition, 2000.

Lin, Cerek. Tao Te Ching: Annotated and Explained. Woodstock: Skylight Paths, 2006.

Mitchell, Stephen. Bhagavad Gita: A New Translation. New York: Three Rivers, 2000.

Neville, Goddard. The Neville Reader. Camarillo: DeVorss, 2011.

Walsch, Neale Donald. Communion with God. New York: Penguin, 2000.

Perricone, Nicholas, M.D. The Perricone Prescription. New York: Harper Collins, 2004.

Ruiz, D. M. The Voice of Knowledge: A Practical Guide to Inner Peace. San Rafael: Amber-Allen, 2004.

Tolle, Eckhart. A New Earth: Awakening to Your Life's Purpose. New York: Penguin, 2006.

Schucman, Helen. A Course In Miracles. New York: Penguin, Foundation for Inner Peace, 1996.

About the Author

Owen Thomas Ashton,
MD, FACPh

Born January 3, 1945, in Wheeling, West Virginia, Dr. Ashton graduated from Ohio State University and immediately entered the U. S. Navy. While on active duty, he completed his Master of Science degree and went on to complete his medical degree at Rush University College of Medicine. He has practiced surgery in Palm Beach Gardens, Florida, since 1984, where he currently resides.

Contact author at
ashtonota@aol.com

Made in the USA
Columbia, SC
29 February 2020

88484868R00133